Russian
mbroidery
lace
.00

146.
37333   22
599 |01438 737599   YEF

Russian
Embroidery
and Lace

L. Yefimova and R. Belogorskaya

Russian Embroidery and Lace

Foreword by Santina Levey

with 191 illustrations, 125 in colour

Thames and Hudson

Frontispiece
Detail of lace bed valance, late 18th
or early 19th century (cf. pl. 58)

Translated from the Russian by Alexandra Ilf

The publishers are grateful for the assistance of
Jennifer Wearden (Embroidery) and Alyson Morris (Lace)
of the Victoria and Albert Museum, London.

First published in Great Britain in 1987 by
Thames and Hudson Ltd, London

Printed and bound in Hungary

Contents

Foreword

Peasant crafts have been admired and studied since the mid-nineteenth century, when efforts were first made to preserve them in the face of increasing industrialization. Many countries showed the products of their craft industries at the great international exhibitions, and Russian lace and embroideries at the Vienna and London Exhibitions of 1873 and 1874 which were given to the South Kensington Museum (now the Victoria and Albert Museum), helped to stimulate the growing interest in lace and embroidery in the Russian style.

Most of the Western copies were based on bobbin-made tape laces in which the tapes were curved back on themselves on either side of a vertical axis to form stylized plant forms. The embroideries were of two main types, both worked by counted thread techniques and both normally employing a red or other monochrome embroidery-thread on a plain linen or cotton ground. In one, the linear designs were worked in double running stitch, and in the other, more solid patterns were worked in cross stitch. In both cases the patterns were either geometric or contained stylized, angular figure motifs. Some Russian drawn threadwork was also copied in the West. In all these cases, the Russian originals were peasant-made pieces of the nineteenth century, but they came to epitomize for many people Russian lace and embroidery as a whole.

In reality, of course, the picture is far more varied, and it is a great pleasure to welcome a book which will introduce English readers to a full range of Russian lace and embroidery. The National Historical Museum in Moscow houses one of the Soviet Union's most important textile collections, and the material drawn from the embroidery and lace sections of the museum illustrates their long and rich history. The earliest surviving embroideries are ecclesiastical; made for the Russian Orthodox Church, they demonstrate the lasting impact of the Byzantine style on Russian art, although the extensive use of pearls gives a distinctive Russian flavour to the later pieces. Pearl embroidery is also a feature of the seventeenth- and eighteenth-century costume items.

By the seventeenth century the Byzantine style had been replaced by a strong Islamic influence. This is particularly noticeable in the metal thread embroideries on velvet grounds, some of which reproduce the effect of Turkish woven velvets with uncanny precision. From the time of Peter the Great, the professional workshops began to make embroideries in the Western style, and all the major trends of the West, including in the nineteenth century the craze for Berlin woolwork, were paralleled in Russia. At the same time, however, Russian peasant dress and embroidery was produced throughout the country. Not only did it have a valid life of its own but it was actively encouraged by the government, and, at the end of the nineteenth century, was being taken up by some Westernized city-dwellers.

Russian lace developed in a similar way. It was introduced from the West and it remained in part a Westernized, fashionable fabric, but it was also assimilated into Russian peasant culture. Thus the typical tape-based bobbin laces, which were made for peasant furnishings and dress into the twentieth century, had their origins in fashionable Milanese lace of the seventeenth century, although the Russian versions are likely to have been based on copies made within the Austro-Hungarian Empire. Less easily recognizable as Russian are the nineteenth-century bobbin laces in the style of Chantilly lace, and the simpler borders which are similar to the products of Buckinghamshire, Tønder and other nineteenth-century centres.

Few Western museums contain examples of Russian lace or embroidery, and those that do are mainly restricted to the more familiar peasant work. It is particularly valuable, therefore, to have this well-illustrated, English-language volume. Textile historians and practising embroiderers and lace-makers alike will find here much to delight and to inspire them.

Santina M. Levey
Victoria and Albert Museum, London

The Embroidery

Twelfth to Early Twentieth Century

The embroidery collection of the Historical Museum, Moscow, is one of the largest and most valuable in the Soviet Union. It comprises several thousand embroidered garments, headdresses, ecclesiastical vestments and church pieces, as well as embroideries for domestic decoration, and it includes the work of both urban and peasant embroiderers.

The collection was started in 1872, the date of the Museum's foundation. It incorporates large and fine collections of embroideries of pre-revolutionary Russia, especially those of P. Shchukin, I. Bilibin, N. Shabelskaya, A. Uvarov and I. Goriainiva. More recent acquisitions of special artistic value are embroidered pieces from Smolensk Province, collected by I. Pogodin, early Russian embroiderers from the Mishukov Collection, and nineteenth-century works by peasant embroiderers from the Strokova Collection. Altogether the collection provides an overview of the best work of Russian embroiderers at every stage of its development.

Early Russian needlework is represented by ecclesiastical and secular embroideries dating from the twelfth to the seventeenth century. The unique pieces of ecclesiastical embroidery, in particular, embody the best traditions of Russian art.

Although there is indirect evidence that a great deal of fine needlework was done in Russia in pagan times, it was Byzantine influence that raised the craft of embroidery to an art. Worked with silk with a flat stitch (as opposed to raised work), embroidery established itself rapidly. By the eleventh century, monasteries in the large towns of Russia possessed their own schools of weaving and embroidery, and imported the finest textiles from East and West to serve as models. The chronicles contain a number of references to the embroideries which adorned the country's chief cathedrals. The textiles which have been preserved, however, are all unpatterned woven fabrics, although some have designs block-printed. The blocks and dyes used during the eleventh century were provided by icon painters, a practice that persisted until the seventeenth century. The designs were often geometric, although some of the earliest surviving examples include patterns of Byzantine and Sassanian origin, while later pieces resemble Italian, Persian and Turkish textile designs.

The influence of the Middle East is evident in the needlework of the early Christian Church in Russia, where ecclesiastical robes glittered with gold thread, and the rich silks of Byzantium were elaborately worked by nuns who learned their craft as part of their general education in the convents. The gold embroidery is among the most sumptuous and delicate needlework ever made. The surviving ecclesiastical vestments of this period are worked with small figures or religious scenes, comparable in style with early Russian manuscript illumination, framed by foliage scrolls or set in geometrical or architectural compartments. These designs are worked with coloured silks in a fine regular split-stitch, generally on backgrounds of couched gold thread.

First, the design to be embroidered was transferred on to the material. Such designs, called cartoons, were either made by the embroiderer himself or commissioned from an artist. The outlines of the cartoon were pricked on to a sheet of paper, which was then laid on the fabric. Powdered charcoal or other such substance, called 'pounce', was rubbed over the paper, so that it passed through the pricked holes and marked the outline on the fabric. The outline design would then be traced with Chinese white or Indian ink.

Several examples of Novgorod embroidery have survived from the twelfth century, and reflect the style of the religious art of the period. A piece in the Historical Museum (pl. 1) is perhaps the earliest of all. It is worked in flat stitch on a fine eleventh-century Byzantine textile woven with designs of Sassanian origin. The rendering of the Crucifixion is linear. The scene is enclosed within a border studded with eleven medallions containing half-figures of Christ, the Evangelists and Apostles. The robes are worked in couched gold and the rest of the scene is in silk. While Byzantine in character, the scene is infused with more expressiveness and movement than is usual in Constantinople work of the same date.

No major examples of thirteenth-century embroidery or textiles have been preserved, but the best Novgorod embroideries from the fourteenth and fifteenth centuries are very fine. Like the earlier panels, they follow the Byzantine tradition, but their style also keeps step with the contemporary Russian religious painting. Flat stitches continue to be used to the exclusion of raised work. To judge by the hangings commissioned by Princess Maria, widow of Semyon the Proud, in 1389 (pl. 2), the backgrounds remained plain. The figures in the Deisis scene are well-proportioned and elegant.

The ground material was generally of silk, and couched gold and silver threads were used for the backgrounds, with figures worked with silks in a fine split-stitch which varied in direction to give an effect of modelling, as where white silk stitches were sewn in concentric circles to suggest the modelling of a cheek. Every detail was executed with an astonishing, minute perfection. Stylistically the embroideries were closely related to contemporary manuscript illuminations, and in some instances the designs were provided by manuscript illuminators. The few sixteenth-century examples are rather on the severe side, with elongated ascetic-looking figures set in delicate patterns of scrollwork. In the seventeenth century a much more elaborate style was developed, with the figures more numerous and crowded, and the overall pattern more closely integrated.

Until the fifteenth century, nuns were responsible for all the important religious panels embroidered in Russia, and they continued until the eighteenth century to provide the greater part of what was embroidered. But in the fifteenth and sixteenth centuries, many fine panels were also made in the sewing-rooms which the ladies of the ruling families established in their palaces. The list of these palace-embroideries is headed by the fine altar cloth showing the Communion of the Apostles (pls. 3–5) worked under the direction of Princess Agrafena between 1410 and 1413 for the Cathedral of the Nativity of the Virgin at Suzdal. Christ appears on it twice, and each time his figure is worked in gold.

By the fifteenth century it was not unusual to place a saint's life-size portrait-icon beside a coffin. Princess Euphrosyne Staritskaya and her embroiderers wor-

Merchant's wife in a *kokoshnik* headdress, 1796

ked a portrait-shroud of Prince Feodor of Yaroslavl (pl. 8). Although the style is iconic and the prince's face ascetic, it probably contains an element of true portraiture. A small number of shrouds of the same type were embroidered during the fifteenth and sixteenth centuries in several princely sewing-rooms.

Embroidered trimmings of similar date decorate the yoke of Abbot Paphnutius' phelonion (pl. 12). Here the needlework sets out to simulate metalwork, with metal plaques to assist the illusion.

Many of the finest large embroideries were produced in the late fifteenth and early sixteenth centuries, when workshops developed a style in which grace and profound piety were combined with stylistic restraint and economy of detail. The style is admirably represented by a panel of a nine-figure Deisis (pls. 6, 7). Each figure standing amidst the ornamentation of simple but charming design is distinguished by a purity and candour of rendering. Like so many fifteenth-century panels this clearly reflects the influence of the painter Andrei Rublev, which was to be followed by that of the painter Dionysius.

In the sixteenth century, backgrounds became more complex, and more use was made of gold and silver thread. As the metal was apt to tear the stuff, it became customary to couch the thread along the fabric, stitching it into place with coloured silks.

Much work of this type was done in palace sewing-rooms and in those which had been established in the households of prominent boyars. Sometimes gems were added, when the embroidery simulated metal-filigree work. Pearl embroidery also became extremely popular at that period. Together with the gold and silver work, this was specially admired by Tsar Boris Godunov (c. 1552–1605). He commissioned several panels as gifts to the Trinity Sergius Monastery near Zagorsk, where they remain to the present day. Since woven patterned fabrics were still extremely expensive and in short supply, plain stuffs were often embroidered to imitate those which were imported (pl. 15).

By the seventeenth century much excellent embroidery was being produced in the major regional capitals, but it was in the workshops which the Stroganovs established at Solvychegodsk that much if the best work was done (pl. 11).

In the late seventeenth century, embroidery with couched gold and silver thread continued in use, but increasingly often patterns were worked all over with coloured silks, using gold thread only for details. The magnificent panels of ecclesiastical vestments were worked with both Oriental and seed pearls, jewels and gold spangles (pls. 26–28). Pearl embroidery was combined not only with gold plaques (cf. pl. 12), but also with jewels, coloured glass beads, gold studs, spangles and heavy bullion (pls. 25–28).

Ornamental embroidery had acquired a special prestige during the sixteenth and seventeenth centuries owing to its use on ecclesiastical vestaments and appurtenances. The costumes of the Russian nobility, too, were worked with gold thread and fine coloured silks, and had seed pearls sewn on the edgings. The Historical Museum's collection of secular embroideries of this period is the most comprehensive in Russia. Most of them are worked with ornamental motifs with a finely

Well-to-do peasant woman in a *kokoshnik* headdress,
first half of 19th century

couched gold thread on a silk ground; several embroidered fragments are worked with coloured silks.

Ornamental embroidery with gold and silver thread is frequently used for the panels of women's garments. Most of such panels are rectangular, with horizontal compositions. Characteristic motifs are animals, birds, foliage and flowers. The stitching is outstanding in its fineness and evenness. Colours are arbitrary rather than realistic, and remarkable effects of relief are obtained by means of texture alone. These panels were regarded as sufficiently precious to figure in inventories and Wills. Many pieces are embroidered with large overall patterns in floss silk; gold thread was couched with silks and used in basket stitch with gold wire. Replicas were made in embroidery of the woven patterns of brocaded silks and velvets imported from both East and West (pls. 14, 15).

The designs include combinations of motifs derived from the Near East, and a large repertory of traditional Russian patterns which represent a totally independent ornamental style, developed in Russia during the sixteenth and seventeenth centuries.

Floral motifs and beasts, such as the panther or lion, appear together with such fabulous creatures as the Sirin, a bird with the head of a woman, and the griffin (pls. 13–19, 24ff.). The depictions are bold and lively, and convey the traditional beliefs which inspired their makers. Much of the decoration has symbolic meaning. Some motifs were originally amulets, protecting against evil—ram's horns, certain birds—or were regarded as bringing good fortune—the sun, the eight-pointed star. The Tree of Life in various forms symbolized the *axis mundi*, or creative centre of the universe; the peacock was a Byzantine symbol of the Resurrection; the unicorn a symbol of purity; the dragon represented fertilizing power, or cosmic energy manifesting in Nature; the griffin was a mythological creature with a lion's body and an eagle's head and wings; the Sirin-bird also represented the favourably aspected heavenly bodies.

Favourite floral motifs are roses, carnations and tulips (pls. 15, 17, 20, 21). Stylized flowers and fabulous beasts are often combined with the Cross or the Tree of Life (pls. 14, 19–24).

Gold embroidered patterns of the late sixteenth and early seventeenth centuries are characterized by axial symmetry. Dense and well-defined areas of colour are set against contrasting grounds. Decorative patterns employed on silks and velvets, while varied, show a predominance of repeat-medallion ornament combined with Sassanian motifs such as confronted winged beasts, birds or lions (pls. 14, 19, 24). Or the design might be less formalized and stiff, being based on an overall pattern of floral medallions with naturalistically represented floral, bird and animal subjects (pls. 13, 15ff.). The overall patterns of gold and silver tracery, generally set against a black or purple velvet ground, produce an effect of great intricacy and richness.

In the second half of the seventeenth century the composition usually includes a central stylized motif flanked by subsidiary elements. The most popular motifs are the pomegranate, a decorative device frequently found in Islamic art, symbolizing fertility and plenty (pls. 17–19, 21), and a large, many-petalled flower with scrolling tendrils bearing leaves and fruit (pls. 20–23). The introduction of printed books in Russia influenced the embroidery designs of the period: the floral and fruit motifs employed sometimes resemble the head-pieces of Moscow printed books (pl. 22).

From the late seventeenth century, the relief elements of the patterns become stronger. Raised work is popular, with relief-embroidery in which human figures and other subjects are worked over shaped blocks of wood or padding, or embroidered separately and then applied to a foundation. Floral and animal motifs of Eastern origin incorporate floral scrolls which terminate in raised fruit and flowers (pl. 23), or confronted griffins and lions flank the Tree of Life motif amid foliage and flowers worked with gold thread, with the field studded with gold spangles (pl. 24). Sometimes the outlines of the patterns are reserved in plain ground material, while the rest of the field is covered with overall stitching in couched gold and silver thread (pl. 22).

A large group of decorative *shirinka* towels (ceremonial towels or kerchiefs) is luxuriously worked with gold and silver thread, coloured silks and pearls, and is trimmed with lace (pls. 30–32). Their ornamentation consists of a repeat motif in the bordering panels, with trailing stems and blossoms, fabulous birds and beasts, and netted fillings, the main motif being a wavy stem carrying symmetrical foliate and floral scrolls. Double-sided stitches are used, so that both surfaces of the embroidery appear alike. The *shirinka* towels are square, and are usually trimmed with deep fringes of silk and gold threads.

A man's shirt of finest linen (pl. 29), modestly ornamented, is a good example of embroidered garments of the late seventeenth century. The lyre-shapes and scroll patterns along the slits are an ancient device for protection against evil, survivals from pre-Christian times.

The embroidery of the northern and central provinces of Russia in the eighteenth and nineteenth centuries, whether in the towns or in peasant communities, shows development in the treatment of traditional motifs. Many different materials and techniques were employed.

Women's headdresses and garments were lavishly worked with seed pearls, couched gold thread, coloured foil sequins and the like (pls. 35–40). The patterns of gold embroidery were outlined with raised stitches for clearer definition.

Gold-thread tracery was predominantly based on schematicized floral and foliate forms, the favourite motifs being large carnations and tulips derived from Islamic art. In the eighteenth century, the motif of a vase or bunch of flowers tied with a ribbon was introduced, and became as popular in embroidery as in other types of folk art (pls. 36–39, 42).

The traditional repertory of ornamental motifs continue in use, although zoomorphic and genre subjects are not often found in gold embroidery (pl. 42). Adapting the subjects in their own way, skilful embroiders created complex, highly schematicized compositions, such as that of a female dancer surrounded by large flowers, with griffins and birds in heraldic pairs (pl. 45), or more formalized compositions, as of a horseman and female spinner, half-hidden in foliate scrolls (pl. 44); the latter subject may be derived from the scenes painted on carved wooden distaffs from the northern Dvina area.

Archaic elements of Russian folk costume survive in patterned *kokoshnik* head-dresses from the Olonetsk Province. The hanging pieces of these headdresses follow the design of metal temple-pendants worn by women from the Slav tribe of Vyatichi between the eleventh and fourteenth centuries.

The headdresses and ornaments worn by peasant women in the northern provinces of Russia (pls. 46–49) were worked with pearls, mother-of-pearl, co-loured glass beads, semi-precious stones and other materials.

The popularity of pearl embroidery in Russia is explained by the ready supply of cheap Russian seed pearls. The most highly valued Oriental pearls were available only for well-to-do peasants and townswomen.

Linen embroidery of the eighteenth century was exceptionally fine. Much of it was drawn threadwork. Threads were drawn from the linen until the fabric resembled a fine gauze, and a pattern was darned on with a coarse linen thread to form geometrical, animal and genre motifs. The narrative character of the compositions (pls. 56, 58, 59) was inspired by Russian folklore, and also by the fine arts of the period. Linen embroidery was usually executed in whitework, i. e. with white thread on a white ground, and was favoured for personal and table linen, bed valances, and the like (pl. 57).

The same type of embroidery made with coloured threads, predominantly with coloured silks, is notable for its delicate colourings, and exquisite foliate and floral motifs. It is closely linked with traditional folk art (pls. 55, 56). The ornamental border of a wedding-sheet (pl. 56) shows a formalized Tree of Life motif flanked by confronted unicorns—symbols of purity—accompanied by archaic geometrical motifs—rosettes, lozenges, saltire crosses, swastikas, etc., once regarded as good luck symbols and talismans.

According to eighteenth-century records, the most popular techniques, fabrics and materials of the period were raised work with gold and silver thread, drawn threadwork embroidered with metal strip, and chain stitch with coloured silks.

The shawls, handkerchiefs, towels, purses and pocket-books in the Museum's collection are worked with white thread on fine muslin and linen, in chain and satin stitches and drawn threadwork.

In the mid-eighteenth century, designs included scrolls, lattices and baskets of flowers. The pieces were worked in satin stitch and long and short stitch, with the addition of heavy bullion, spangles and applied net.

In the late eighteenth century, beneath the man's coat was worn a waistcoat of different material, sometimes heavily embroidered; later the embroidery spread to the coat itself (pl. 61). There developed a custom of further embellishing embroideries with sewn-on glass beads and bird's feathers. In the 1780s the asymmetry of Rococo gave way to a strict axial symmetry and to motifs mainly of classical origin, which were applied, wherever the neoclassical style penetrated, on embroidery, furniture, ceramics, textiles, metalwork, and for interior decora-

Merchant's wife in a *kokoshnik* headdress,
first half of 19th century

tion generally, creating an elegance based on straight lines and geometrical balance.

In the eighteenth century embroidered pictures became popular, apparently after the emergence of printed pattern-books. The fashion coincided with the rise of domestic embroidery, and the idea that needlework belonged peculiarly to the province of women of leisure. The scenes copied were frequently landscapes, sometimes in the Chinese style, or the designs might imitate bird- or flower-paintings. The embroidered picture illustrated (pl. 83) was worked by the wife of a noted Russian poet, Derzhavin. Satin and cross stitch were almost exclusively employed, and couched gold thread was largely abandoned.

The art of quilting, always largely a folk art, is represented by splendid coverlets and petticoats dating from the second half of the eighteenth century. The lines of stitches were often curved into shells or scrolls, and these shapes were combined into more intricate designs. Overall patterns were made from a basic feather motif, and several patterns were sometimes worked on one quilt (pl. 76). Quilts were frequently ornamented in addition with embroidery or patchwork, and surrounded by an elaborate border. Such luxurious quilts were often mentioned in inventories, and became family heirlooms.

In the 1790s fashion took on a new, 'classical' simplicity. Women wore the 'Empire gown', also called a *robe en chemise*, which consisted of a white, high-waisted garment falling to the feet, in soft fabrics such as spot muslins and transparent lawns. Fine silks and satins took the place of the stiffened velvets, heavy brocades and damasks which had been popular for so many years. Ribbons and unstarched lace, white or in paler and more delicate colours, succeeded the rather harsh brilliance of an earlier period. Embroidery on fine nettings and muslins now reached a high level of skill. Dresses made of crêpe were worked with gold spangles. The hems of women's dresses were decorated with raised work and appliqué. Designs were accented with beads, spangles and silk-wrapped gimp or chenille (pls. 63–69). Drawn from the peasant tradition were designs of coloured embroidery with indigenous plant forms (pls. 67, 69).

In the nineteenth century embroidery was much used for rugs (pl. 87), screens, purses, reticules and pocket-books (pls. 84–86), and the like, worked in a variety of materials and techniques. Decoration of pocket books with hair (pl. 84) simulated the effect of a line-engraving. Beadwork came into vogue. Popular were cross stitch with coloured thread on an openwork ground, and satin stitch. Household linen and costumes were decorated with whitework, chain stitch and filet network, and with broderie anglaise of geometrical or stylized floral patterns. Gold embroidery continued in use during the nineteenth and into the twentieth century, retaining its traditional forms and styles, but became the prerogative of the ruling classes.

During the second half of the nineteenth century, embroidery spread to outerwear—mantles, cloaks and tippets. Incorporated into the patterns were cord, pastes or applied fabrics.

In the last quarter of the nineteenth century, with the coming of the machine

Merchant's wife in a *kokoshnik* headdress,
first half of 19th century

age, embroidery techniques and craftsmanship entered a period of decline. Peasant embroidery, however, which owed little to outside influences, continued to flourish, and the level of skill remained high.

The Museum's nineteenth- and early twentieth-century peasant embroidery collection is an important one. It is remarkable for the immensely rich ornamentation, derived from unique and deeply rooted local traditions. Russian folk embroidery retains many archaic elements, survivals from the beliefs of earlier times. It represents the unbroken expression of a culture.

The collection includes clothing, headdresses, valances, table-cloths, the *shirinka* towels, ceremonial towels carried at weddings and other religious and family occasions, and so on, as well as separate embroidered panels. The largest group comes from the northern provinces (Archangel, Vologda, Novgorod and Tver).

In the northern provinces linen was embroidered with cotton and linen threads, or occasionally with silk and wool. Designs were worked in red on a white ground to produce a bold and bright effect. Especially popular were panels decorated with coloured threads in satin stitch, and counted thread work forming geometrical patterns. The composition consisted of up to three sections with a large figure in the centre. The traditional arrangement focused attention on the most important symbolic or religious object by presenting it in the centre. Sometimes the central image was flanked by a pair of beasts, confronted or back-to-back, or small designs that created a chequered pattern. Common were rows of repeating or alternating motifs. The conventional motifs—a stylized Tree of Life, a horse and rider, a female figure with arms raised, fabulous beasts and birds, architectural, plant and geometric forms—were common to all Russian folk art.

Also illustrated among the plates are equally traditional but rarer subjects which have their origin in Slav pagan mythology (pls. 88–96). Such a survival is the Sirin – the bird with the head of a woman which lured travellers to their doom with the beauty of its song (pls. 90, 92). The Sun is represented by a horse and rider, and is accompanied by a figure with both arms raised, possibly the Earth Goddess. The unicorn, panther and a wide range of plant forms are of Eastern origin. Designs reflecting agrarian rites and customs are naturally prominent. Embroideries have provided archaeologists and ethnographers such as V. Gorodtsov, Acad. Rybakov and G. Maslova with rich material for study.

The techniques of peasant embroidery offer a large repertory, permitting harmonius blending of materials and colours. Chain stitch with coloured thread on a calico foundation was popular in the northern provinces at the end of the last century and the early years of this. It was used for traditional motifs and embroidered scenes (pls. 112, 114).

Embroideries produced in the southern provinces (Tambov, Voronezh, Kaluga and Tula) are typically geometrical, ranging from simple linear motifs to complex multiple designs (pls. 116–120). The stylization, even of floral motifs, is extreme. Such geometrical imagery once held symbolic or magical meaning, and geometric patterns in embroidery, as in woodcarving, can be traced back to the earliest surviving examples of folk art.

Figurative designs, also, were popular in the southern provinces during the period. These did not adhere to the conventions of composition followed in the northern provinces, the elements of the design being more freely disposed over the area of the pattern.

The embroidery of the southern provinces is remarkable for the richness of its colour-schemes. Pieces are worked with wool in strong colours. In the Tambov and Voronezh Provinces the designs were usually outlined with black cotton thread (pl. 122). To the colourful ornamentation of men's and women's festive shirts in the Voronezh Province was added gold lace and calico insertions. The hems of *poniova* petticoats were lavishly decorated with coloured wool embroidery. Sometimes the petticoats were covered with an overall embroidered design; or a woven checked fabric might have the pattern outlined with raised work.

With the advance of industrialization, urban influences reached peasant communities, gradually eroding local craft traditions. Especially in the southern provinces, the traditional designs, embroidered in so many techniques for so long, were almost entirely supplanted by naturalistic patterns of flowers crudely executed in red and black cross stitch.

The embroidered pieces illustrated in this volume are remarkable for their sheer beauty, but also for their historical value, reflecting as they do craft traditions extending over eight centuries. They offer a rich source of inspiration to modern embroiderers, and to artists and craft-workers in other media also.

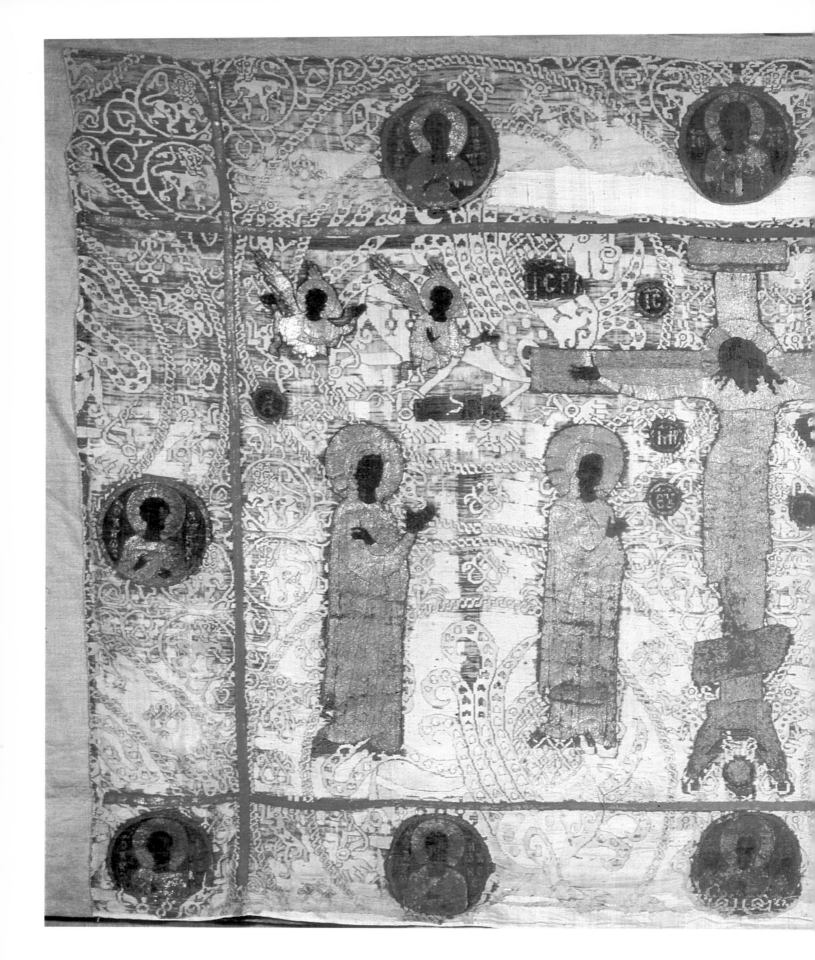

1 Altar frontal with the Crucifixion and Interceding Saints,
Novgorod,
12th century

2 Altar frontal with the Vernicle and Interceding Saints,
Moscow,
1389

3 Altar frontal with the Eucharist, known as the Suzdalian Shroud,
Moscow,
1410–13

4   Border scene from the Suzdalian Shroud

5   Border scene from the Suzdalian Shroud

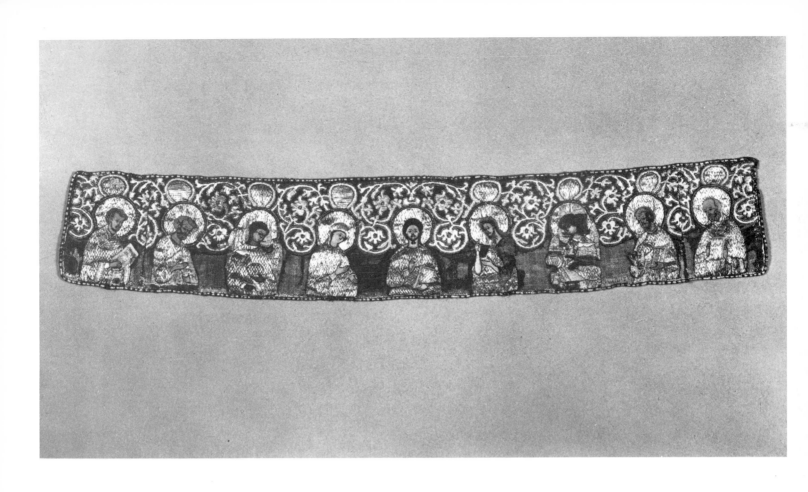

6, 7 (Top) Panel with the Deisis,
Moscow, late 15th or early 16th century.
(Above) Detail

8   Pall with figures of Prince Feodor of Yaroslavl
    and his sons David and Constantine,
    Moscow, 1501

9 Shroud with the Assumption of the Virgin,
known as 'The Cloudy Assumption'.
From the sewing-rooms of Princess Staritsky, 1560s

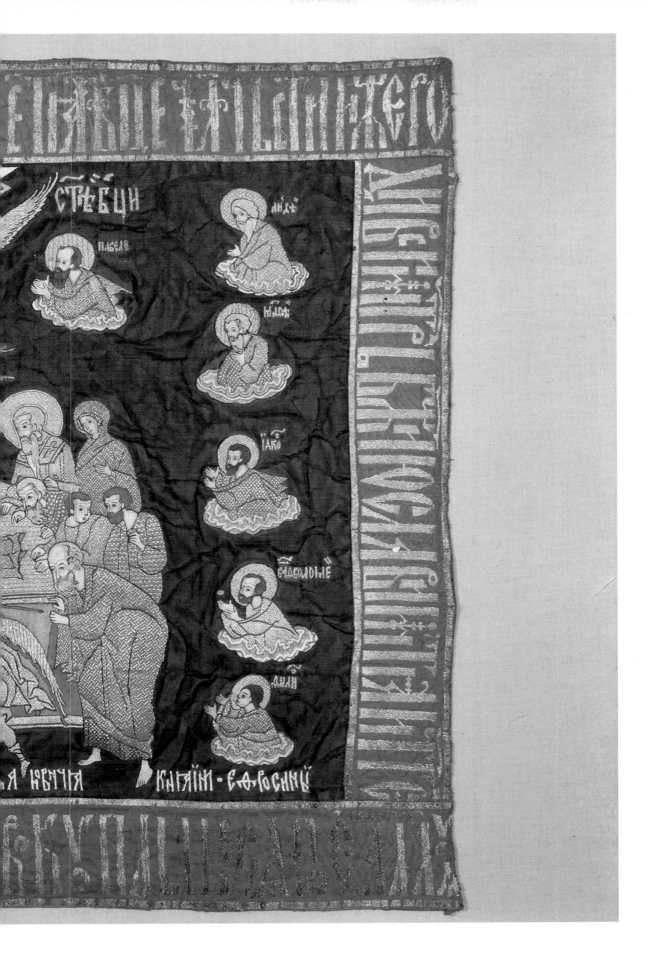

10 Icon of St Sophia, Divine Wisdom,
Moscow,
early 16th century

11   Icon with figures of Saints Zosima and Savvaty.
From the sewing-rooms of the Stroganovs,
Solvychegodsk, second half of 17th century

12 Pearl-embroidered yoke of a phelonion,
15th century

13 Panel embroidered with gold and silver thread,
16th—17th century

14 (Top) Sleeve-band detail embroidered with
gold and silver thread,
late 16th or early 17th century

15 (Above) Detail of yoke of a phelonion,
embroidered with gold and silver thread,
late 16th or early 17th century

16 Panel embroidered with gold and silver thread,
    17th century

17 Sleeve-band embroidered with gold and silver thread,
17th century

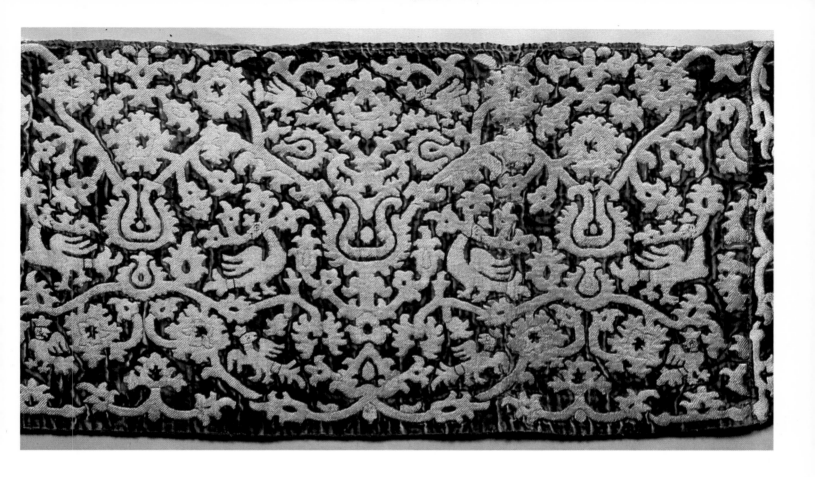

18, 19 Two panels embroidered with gold and silver thread,
17th century

20 Panel embroidered with gold and silver thread,
second half of 17th century

21 Panel embroidered with gold and silver thread,
second half of 17th century

22　Panel embroidered with gold and silver thread,
　　second half of 17th century

23 Yoke of a phelonion,
    embroidered with gold and silver thread,
    late 17th century

24 Panel embroidered
    with gold and silver thread,
    undated

25 Pearl-embroidered
     woman's headdress,
     17th century

26 Pearl-embroidered edging
     of liturgical cuffs,
     late 17th or early 18th century

27 Pearl-embroidered yoke of ecclesiastical vestment,
late 17th or early 18th century

28 Pearl-embroidered yoke of ecclesiastical vestment,
late 17th or early 18th century

29 Man's shirt,
17th century

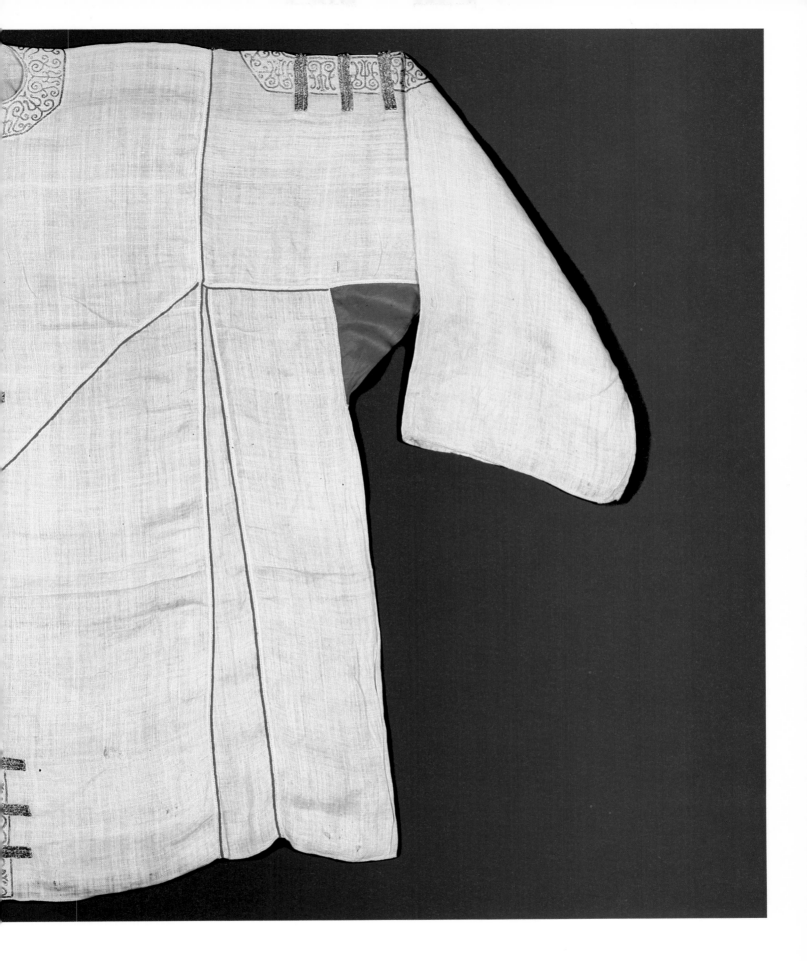

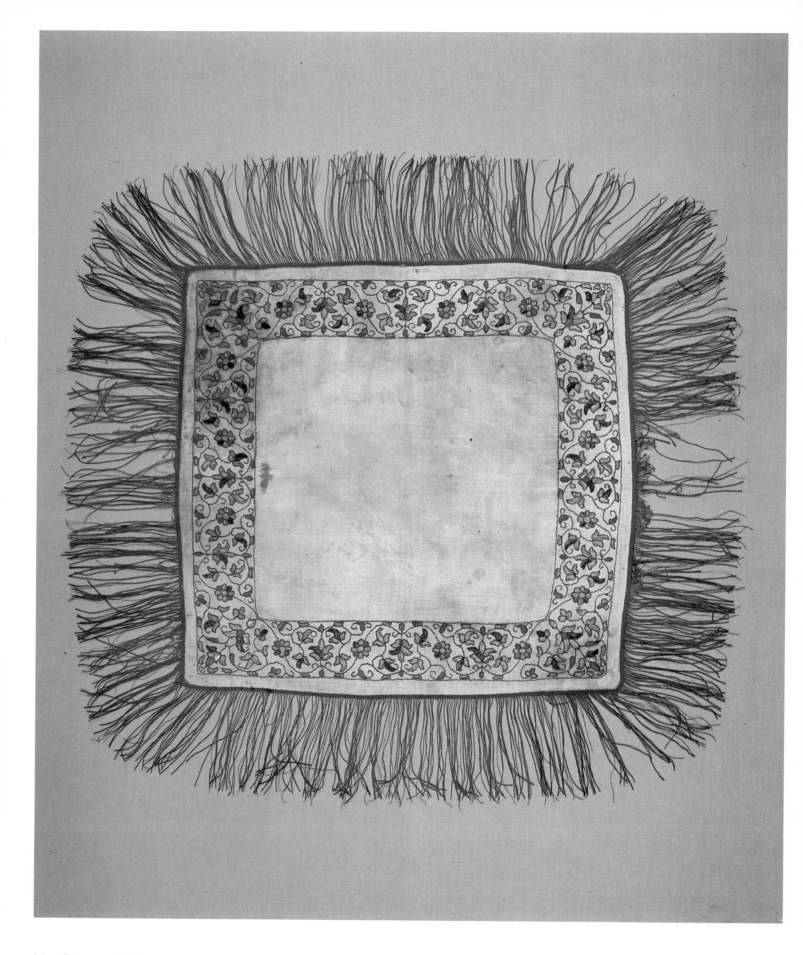

30 Ceremonial *shirinka* towel,
17th century

31 (Top) Ceremonial *shirinka* towel, 17th century

32 (Above) Fragment of ceremonial *shirinka* towel, late 17th or early 18th century

33, 34   Details of gold-embroidered panel,
first half of 18th century

35 Top of *kokoshnik* headdress,
Moscow Province, second half of 18th century

36 Back of *kokoshnik* headdress,
Central Russia,
second half of the 18th century

37 Back of *kokoshnik* headdress,
Central Russia,
late 18th century

38 Back of *kokoshnik* headdress,
Central Russia,
second half of 18th century

39 *Kokoshnik* headress,
Moscow Province,
early 19th century

40   Fragment of cloak with gold embroidery,
     second half of 18th century

41 Reticule (centre) and two purses embroidered with gold and silver thread,
    late 18th or early 19th century

42   Gold-embroidered sleeve of woman's blouse,
     Tver Province,
     late 18th or early 19th century

43 Back of woman's jacket embroidered with gold and silver thread,
Nizhny Novgorod Province,
late 18th or early 19th century

44   Back of *kokoshnik* headdress,
      Olonetsk Province,
      late 18th or early 19th century

45 Back of *kokoshnik* headdress,
late 18th or early 19th century

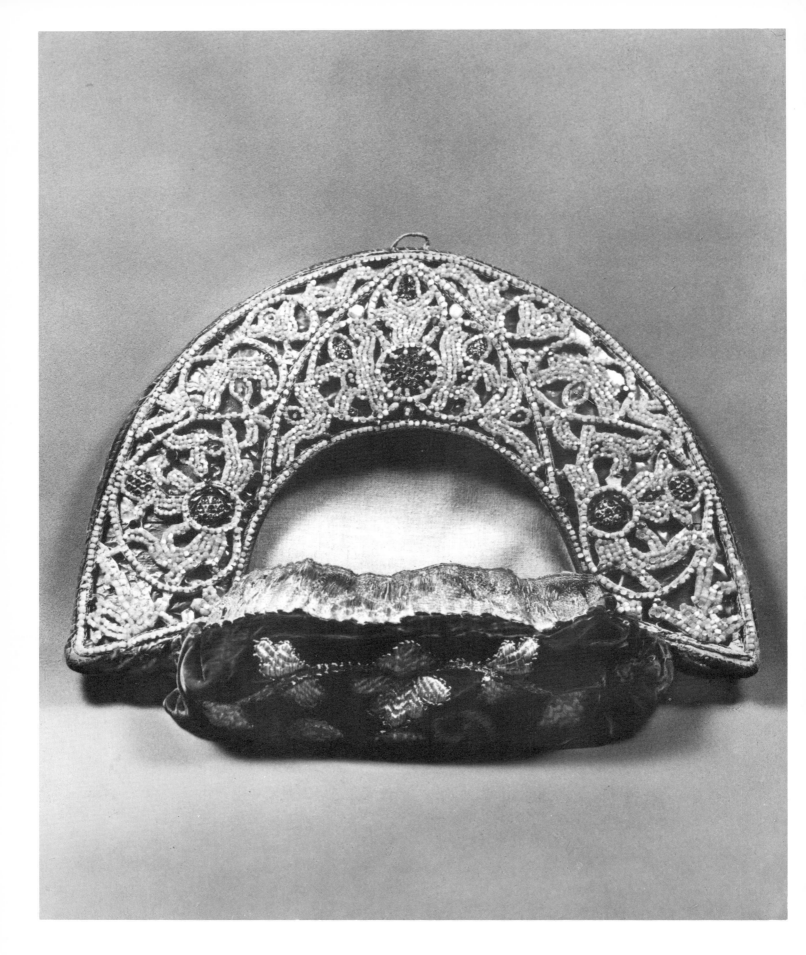

46 Pearl-embroidered *kokoshnik* headdress,
Central Russia,
late 18th or early 19th century

47 Pearl-embroidered *kokoshnik* headdress,
Pskov Province,
late 18th or early 19th century

48 Pearl-embroidered headdress of unmarried peasant girl,
    Vologda Province,
    early 19th century

49 Pearl-embroidered women's headdresses,
Tver Province,
late 18th or early 19th century

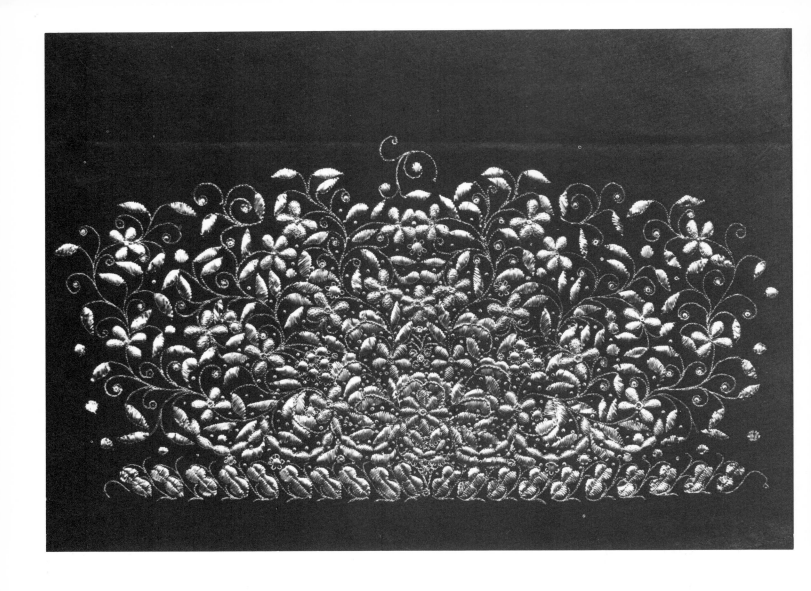

50 Shawl border embroidered with gold and silver thread,
    Nizhny Novgorod Province,
    19th century

51 Gold-embroidered festive shawl,
    Nizhny Novgorod,
    late 18th or early 19th century

52 Gold-embroidered corner of festive shawl,
Olonetsk Province,
1882

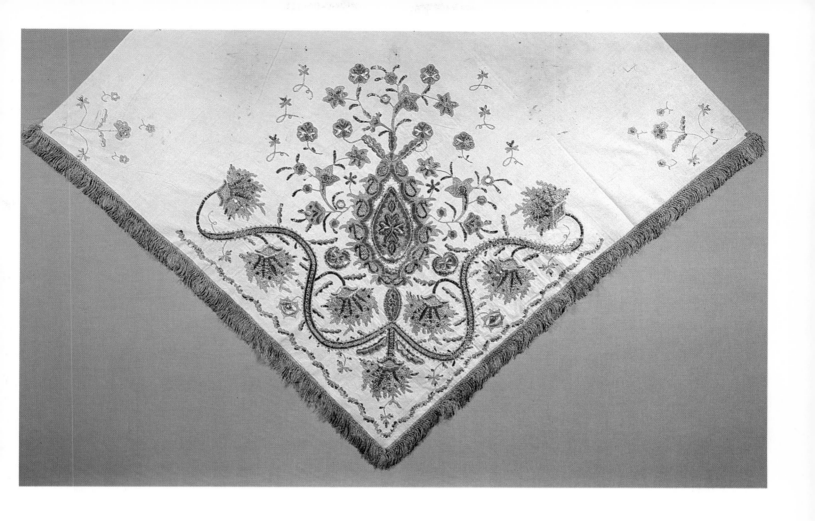

53 Gold-embroidered corner of festive shawl,
    Olonetsk Province,
    1900s

54 (Top) Detail of bed valance,
    Kostroma Province,
    late 18th or early 19th century

55 (Above) Towel edge,
    Kostroma Province,
    early 19th century

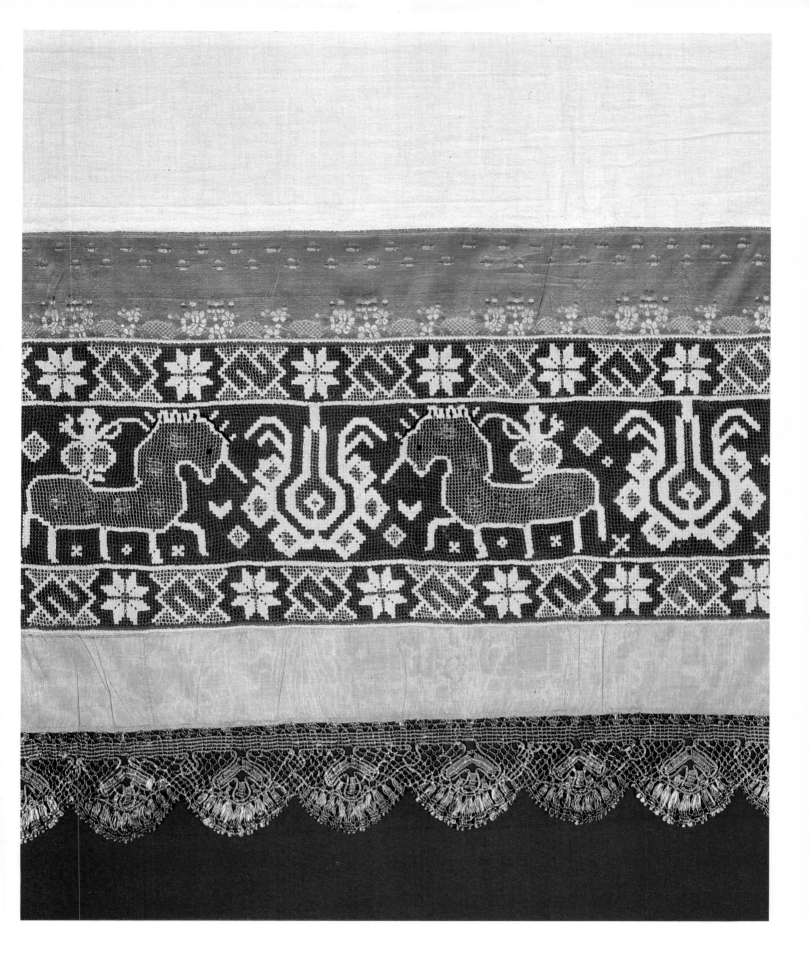

56   Bed valance,
     Tver Province,
     18th century

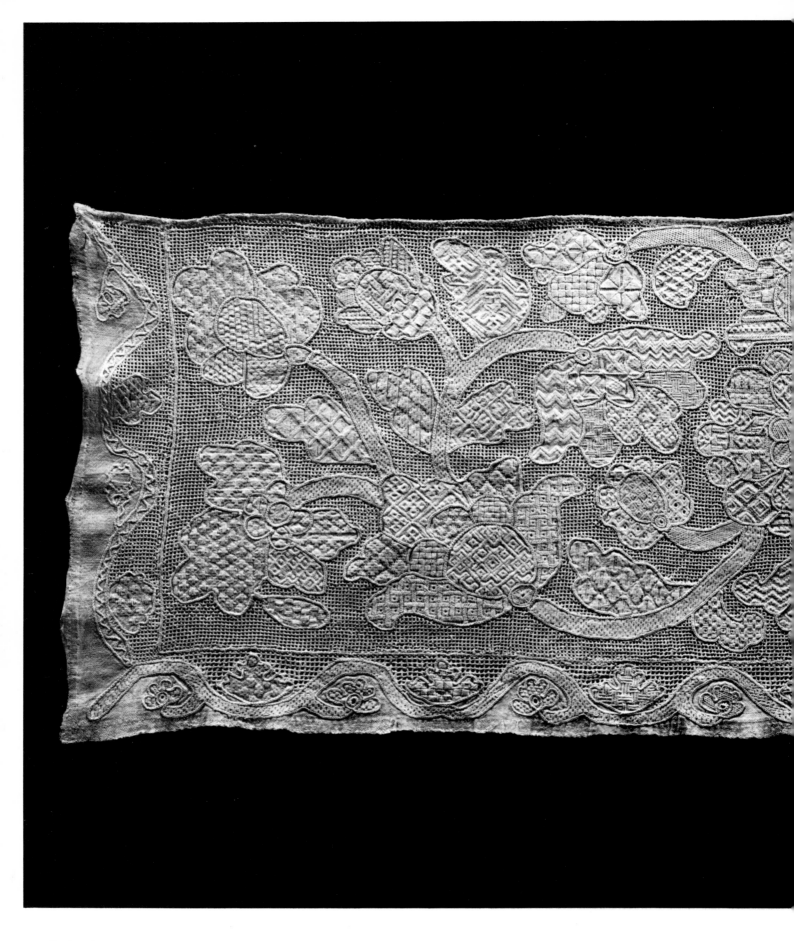

57 Bed valance,
Archangel Province(?),
18th century

58   (Top) Bed valance,
       late 18th or early 19th century

59   (Above) Bed valance,
       Yaroslavl Province,
       late 18th century

60 Detail of panel,
late 18th century

61 Detail of man's coat,
    late 18th century

62 Detail of petticoat,
second half of 18th century

63   Detail of dress,
     mid-18th century

64 Hem of ball-dress,
    late 18th century

65   Hem of ball-dress,
     last quarter of 18th century

66　Hem of ball-dress,
last quarter of 18th century

67 (Top) Hem of ball-dress, 1810s

68 (Above) Hem of dress, late 18th or early 19th century

69 Hem of ball-dress,
1810s

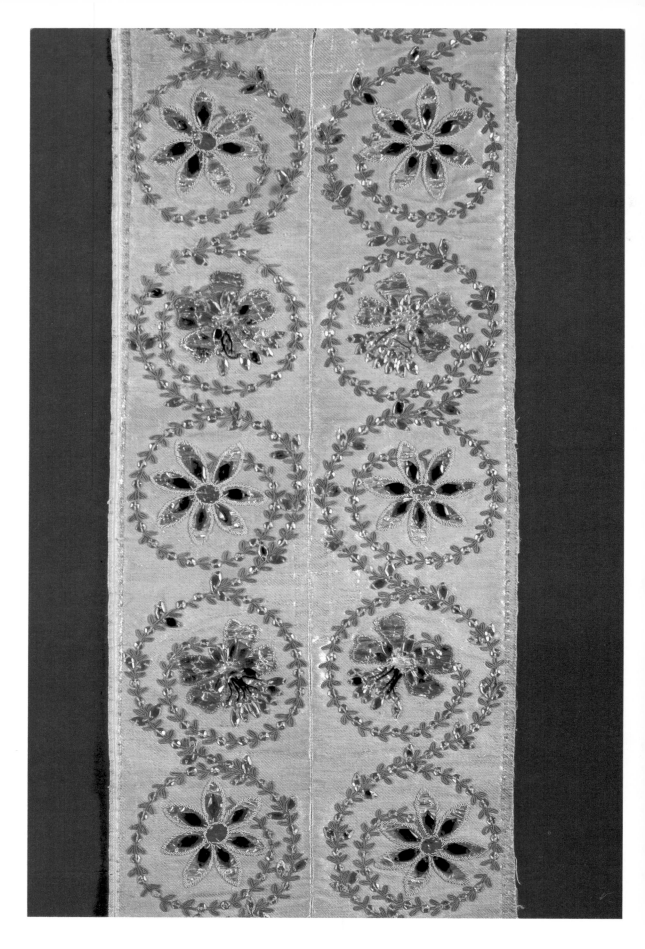

70　Detail of panel,
　　last quarter of 18th century

71 Detail of door-curtain,
    late 18th or early 19th century

72 (Top) Handkerchief,
    last quarter of 18th century

73 (Above) Handkerchief,
   late 18th century

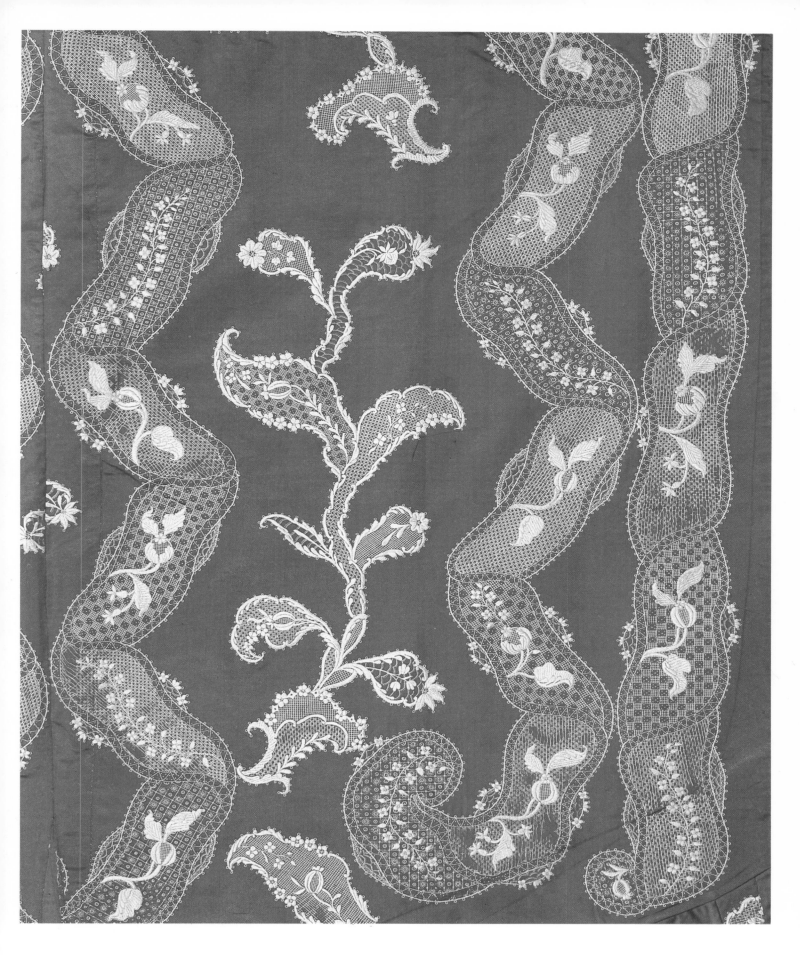

74 Detail of panel,
    second half of 18th century

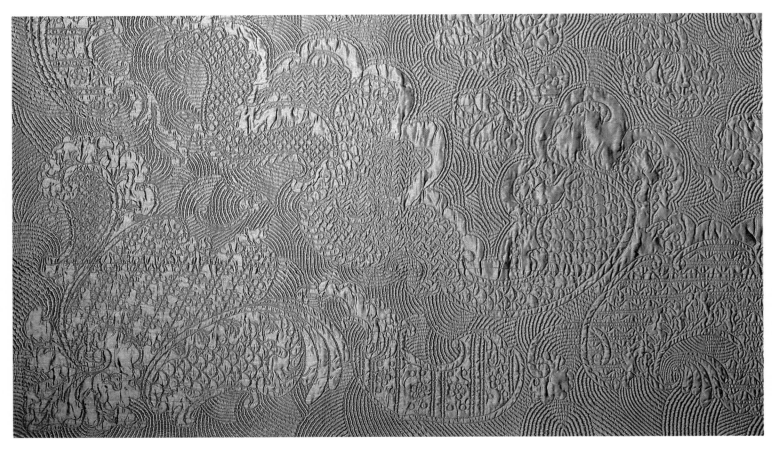

75 (Top) Detail of quilted bed coverlet, 18th century

76 (Above) Detail of quilted bed coverlet, mid-18th century

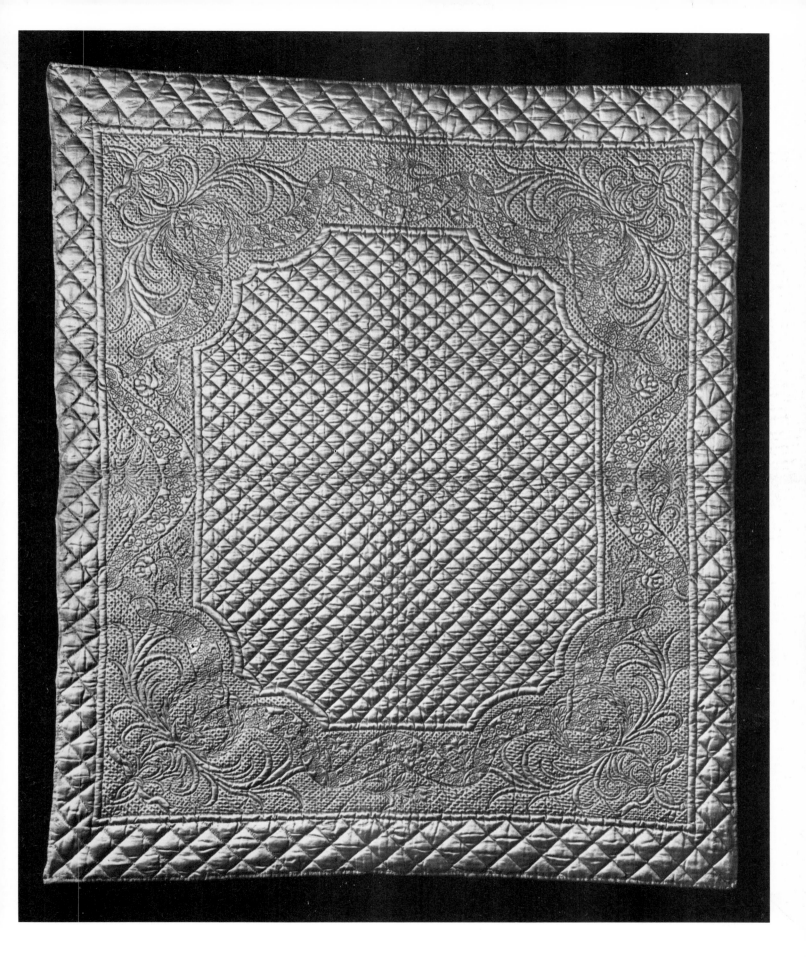

77 Child's quilted bed coverlet,
second half of 18th century

78 Gold-embroidered towel edge,
late 18th century

79 Towel edge,
    early 19th century

80 Towel edge,
late 18th or early 19th century

81, 82 (Top) Wedding-sheet edge. (Above) Detail.
Nizhny Novgorod Province,
second half of 19th century

ШИЛА КАТЕГИНА ДЕРЖАВИНА 1782 ГОДУ.

83 Embroidered scene,
1782

84 Pocket-book cover,
first quarter of 19th century

85 Pocket-book cover,
    mid-19th century

86 Pocket-book cover,
first half of 19th century

87 Embroidered rug,
late 19th century

88 Towel edge,
Olonetsk Province,
mid-19th century

89 Towel edge,
Nizhny Novgorod Province,
mid-19th century

90 (Top) Bed valance, 91 (Above) Hem of skirt (detail),
   Olonetsk Province,   Olonetsk Province,
   mid-19th century   1848

92 Sirin-birds and Alcanoste,
detail of bed valance
(cf. pl. 90)

93 (Top) Detail of valance,
Novgorod Province,
mid-19th century

94 (Above) Towel edge,
Vologda Province,
late 19th century

95 (Top) Table-cloth edge,
    Tver Province,
    late 19th century

96 (Above) Wedding-sheet edge,
    Novgorod Province,
    mid-19th century

97 Towel edge,
    Tver Province,
    1900s

98 Towel edge,
Tver Province,
late 19th or early 20th century

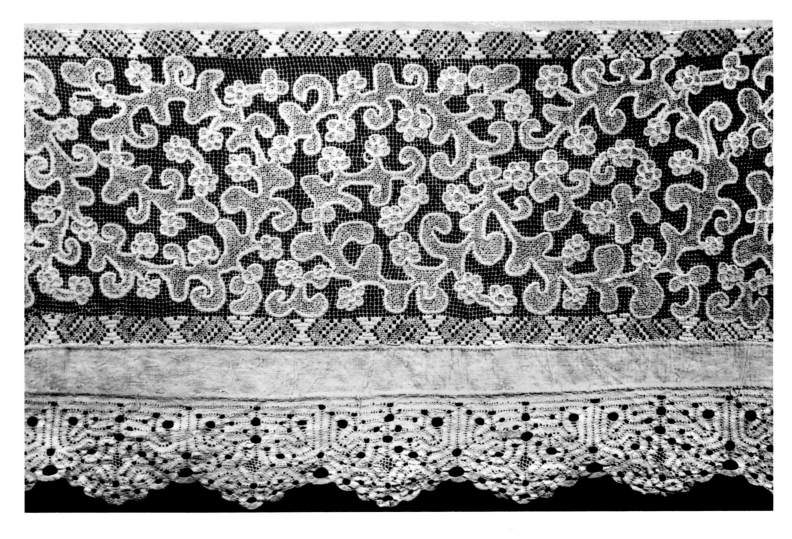

99 (Top) Shoulder-piece of woman's blouse,
    Olonetsk Province,
    mid-19th century

100 (Above) Detail of bed valance,
     mid-19th century

101 Towel edge,
Yaroslavl Province (?),
early 19th century

102 Towel edge,
second half of 19th century

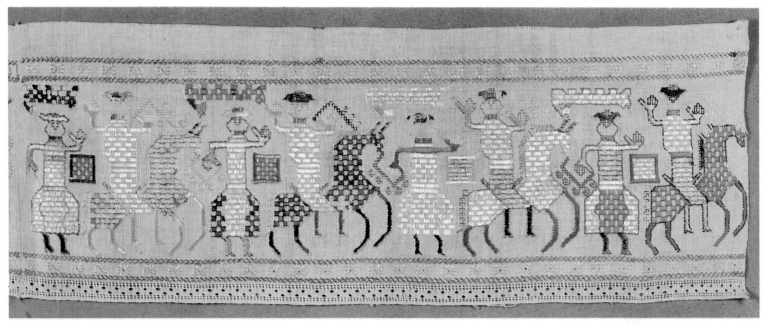

103 (Top) Towel edge,
Pskov Province,
mid-19th century

104 (Above) Detail of table-cloth edging,
19th century

105 Towel edge,
Vologda Province,
late 19th century

106 Towel edge,
Archangel Province,
early 20th century

107 Fabrics for sleeves of women's shirts,
Archangel, Vologda and Olonetsk Provinces,
second half of 19th century

108 Apron, Vologda Province,
     second half of 19th century

109 Apron, Archangel Province,
second half of 19th century

110   Detail of bed valance
       Tver Province,
       mid-19th century

111 Towel edge,
Vologda Province,
late 19th century

112 Towel edge,
Olonetsk Province,
late 19th or early 20th century

113   Apron hem,
       Olonetsk Province,
       1900s

114 Detail of bed valance,
Olonetsk Province,
early 20th century

115 Detail of hem insertion,
     Olonetsk Province,
     1900s

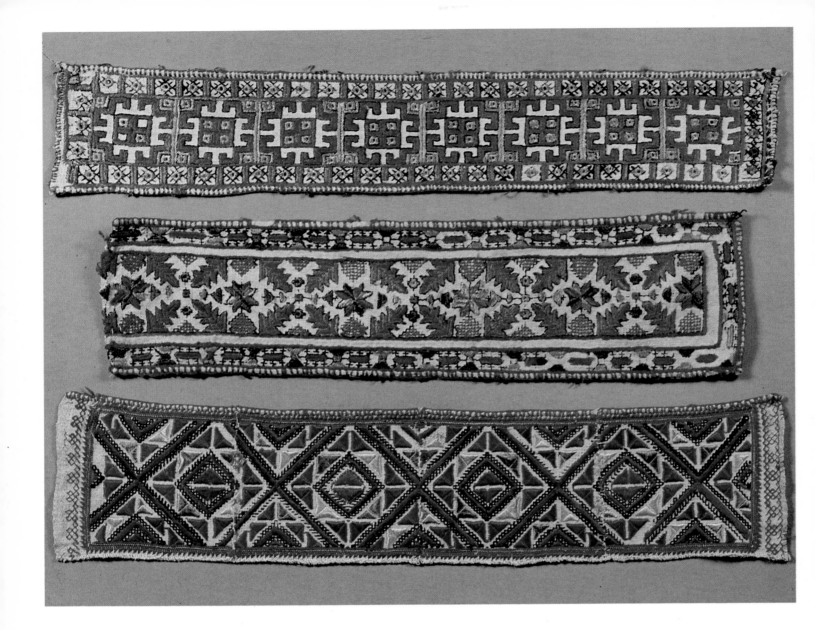

116 Samplers,
Tambov Province,
second half of 19th century

117 Samplers,
Voronezh Province,
second half of 19th century

118 Sampler,
Tambov or Voronezh Province,
second half of 19th century

119   Detail of peasant petticoat,
       Orel Province,
       early 20th century

120 Sarafan,
Kharkov Province,
second half of 19th century

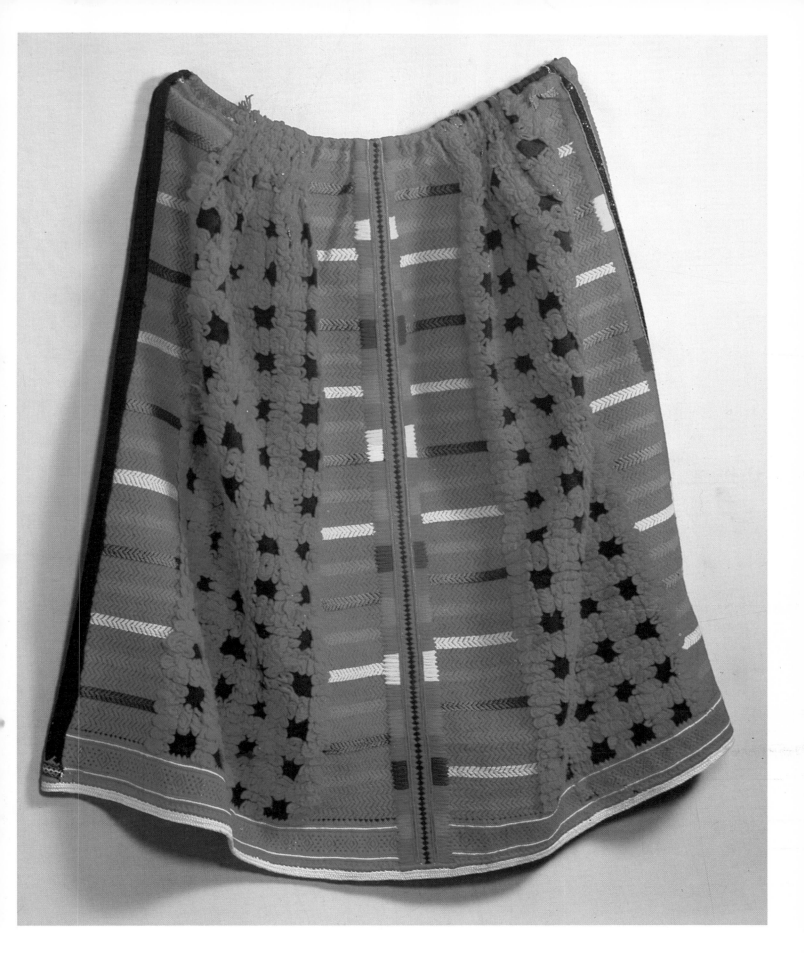

121 Petticoat,
Voronezh Province,
late 19th or early 20th century

122 Back of woman's shirt,
Voronezh Province,
early 20th century

The Lace

*Seventeenth to Early
Twentieth Century*

Page 148
Detail of sheet valance (cf. pl. 158)

The Historical Museum houses a comprehensive collection of Russian lace, with its nucleus in the Shchukin Collection acquired between 1905 and 1911. After the October Revolution of 1917 the Museum collection was augmented from the State Museum Reserve with laces that were received from former churches, monasteries and re-organized museums. Further pieces have been acquired through the Museum Purchasing Commission. The collection includes lace of gold and silver thread produced in the seventeenth and eighteenth centuries, and lace of cotton, linen and silk of the eighteenth, nineteenth and early twentieth centuries.

Bobbin lace has been the only type of lace-making practised in Russia. It is made with a number of threads, each wound on a bobbin easily held in the hand. A pattern is drawn on parchment or stiff paper, and holes are pricked to indicate where pins will be placed to keep the thread in position while the lace is being made. This pricking is fixed to a pillow, and the threads with the bobbins hanging on them are fastened to the pricking at the beginning of the pattern. In working the lace, each hand holds a pair of bobbins which are twisted and interchanged in various ways to form the different structures—cloth stitch, 'wheat-grains', mesh ground, and so on.

There are two types of bobbin lace. One type is straight lace, in which the pattern and ground are worked together as a single piece. The width of a straight lace is limited by the size of the pillow, and the work proceeds from the top of the pillow down towards the worker. The second type is free lace, or tape lace, in which the pattern is worked first and the ground is added afterwards. In a piece of free lace, the main elements of the design (generally flower or leaf motifs, but sometimes human figures, animals, etc.) are made from a tape or braid, and are sometimes outlined with thicker thread to introduce relief. The worker can turn the pillow to the most convenient angle, following the design as the work progresses. The design elements are joined by bars called brides (either plain or decorated with picots) or by a regular mesh or net ground.

The outer, or shaped, edge of the lace is called the head side and the firm, straight edge by which the lace is sewn to a garment is known as the footside.

As well as patterns made on a pricking, there are simple patterns which can be learned by heart, employed particularly in peasant lace-making.

The earliest Russian lace is not well documented, but from the seventeenth century onwards, lace of gold and silver thread was in abundant use for both masculine and feminine costume, and laces as well as embroidery were in constant demand with the well-to-do. Gold and silver lace were highly valued because the threads themselves were costly; the lace was even sold by weight.

The Muscovy Company was the first to import gold and silver lace to Moscow. Ivan IV the Terrible (1530–1584) and Boris Godunov (c. 1552–1605) were quick to trim their finest robes with it, in place of locally produced braids and embroidery. Merchants imported a rich variety of luxurious woven fabrics, fine silks, velvets, damasks, and lace, which found a ready market; and although the quantity of lace imported rapidly increased, after twenty-five years production began in the sewing-rooms of the Armoury in the Moscow Kremlin. By 1627 it was also being made in the Stroganov sewing-rooms in Solvychegodsk, and by the middle of the century so largely was it produced that a cheaper variety made of copper thread could be bought in the Moscow markets.

The chief application of gold and silver lace was to decorate costume; its elaborate richness made it especially suitable for ecclesiastical and ceremonial uses. As a mark of prestige, it decorated the Tsar's throne, boyars' tapestries, armchairs, saddles, and the like, while in churches it bordered shrouds and chalice covers. Gold and silver lace perfectly complemented imported Eastern and Western luxurious gold brocades and embroideries.

The lace might be made either of gold and silver thread alone, or of gold and silver thread whipped over with coloured silks, the motifs being outlined by a series of small picots in metal thread. It was usually a straight lace, forming a braid of variable width with fancy edges. Sometimes the scallops in turn had zig-zag or toothed edgings. Often pearls, sequins and coloured stones were worked into lace, with the heavier varieties used as bed-hangings, the more delicate as dress-trimmings.

During the same period, Russian lace-makers who were engaged in copying Flemish lace produced floral designs which often featured tulips and carnations, with the tulip motif sometimes so schematized as to become virtually an abstract design element. Others copied the geometrical patterns typical in Italian laces.

In the eighteenth and early nineteenth centuries, lace was lavishly applied to court and ceremonial dress like coronation mantles and tippets, and ladies' blouses were covered with decorative nettings of gold and silver mesh. A scarf of silver lace (pl. 134) provides a most attractive example of a large-scale, geometricized foliate design.

Galloons of gold and silver thread were widely used during the eighteenth century. They consisted of a braid with identical scallops along both borders. The patterns were often formed of an undulating line with small circle motifs, or alternating plant and fan motifs (pl. 131). Occasionally a coloured metal strip, common in Russian embroidery, was introduced for added brilliance.

The technical mastery of the period is best seen in specimens decorated with squares and diamond-shapes, with various ornamental fillings and relief effects. The grounds had regular meshes decorated with tiny picots. Typical is an insertion made of silver lace (pl. 133), its pattern based on large diamonds with plain or toothed outlines and smaller diamonds containing rosettes. The ground mesh is regular and clearly defined in heavier silver thread. Such patterns were also widely popular in nineteenth-century peasant lace.

Following Peter the Great's Westernizing reforms in the eighteenth century there developed an almost insatiable demand for thread lace, with which the garments of both men and women were lavishly ornamented in accordance with the new European style. Popular was delicate linen lace with a ground of finest thread. Before 1800 the threads were usually of linen; after that date cotton was more usual. Lace of combined silk and metal threads was also made, the silk thread

Portrait of Anna Nikolayevna, a Kalmuck Woman, 1767

giving a softer effect of shot gold. The gold thread itself became thinner. Exquisite colour-schemes enhanced graceful designs consisting of more naturalistic and highly decorative floral forms. Alongside these, however, we still find continuing the ancient motifs of confronted animals and birds at either side of a Tree of Life. Later, one may detect a progression from a naturalistic treatment towards greater emphasis on abstract and decorative values. Fabulous beasts eventually merged with the floral designs to create elaborate patterns.

In laces of fine texture the motifs continued to be outlined in gold thread, with the rest of the design worked in coloured silk, linen or cotton thread. Towards the end of the eighteenth century, lace of gold and silver thread was gradually abandoned, the gold serving only as an outlining thread, and employed in peasant festive costume exclusively, to decorate *kokoshnik* headdresses, dresses known as *sarafans,* short, waisted garments with a peplum known as *dushegreya* jackets, and the like.

Patterns of European derivation were remarkably naturalistic roses, carnations and daisies on a fine net ground, either as single blossoms or gathered into delicate arrangements, while borders were filled with elaborate patterns or light garlands.

In eighteenth-century Russia, lace had generally been made by serfs. Often rich landowners in remote provinces sent their peasants to lace-making centres to be taught the craft. Around the turn of the century the lace-making industry was established on a large scale. A manufactory owned by Prince Kurakin in the Orel Province, for instance, had in 1814, ninety-three craftswomen making net lace suitable for bed linen, caps, bonnets, scarves and veils. Fashionable types of lace were produced there, imitating Chantilly, Valenciennes, blonde and Mechlin laces, which in the manufactory account-books are called 'French lace'.

Mechlin-type laces of finest linen thread were produced in the first decades of the nineteenth century by serf lace-makers in the Kherson Province (pls. 176, 177). This lace is readily distinguished by the presence of a slightly thicker glossy thread outlining the motifs. The ground is commonly hexagonal, but was often varied, with some decorative effects. Patterns include flowers, sprigs and leaves. The graceful, elegant designs illustrated in the plates are characteristic.

A high reputation was won by Russian blonde lace, a very fine silk lace with a hexagonal mesh using two different thicknesses of filmy floss silk, originally a natural cream-colour but later black. Each element of the pattern is outlined with a thicker strand of flat untwisted silk, instead of the more usual twisted thread. Blonde lace was made in strips a few inches wide which were joined to produce large articles such as shawls, head-coverings, sleeves, kerchiefs, even dresses. They were made by skilful lace-makers in Moscow and St Petersburg, and in lace-making centres such as that at Balakhna in the Nizhny Novgorod Province. Their quality was so high that Russian-made blonde or Chantilly lace was difficult to distinguish from lace made in Western Europe (pls. 164, 178–180).

From the mid-eighteenth century onwards and particularly in the nineteenth century, bobbin lace was in demand at many social levels, and especially for the increasingly prosperous merchants and bourgoisie.

Portrait of S. Vishniakova, *née* Cherokova, 1821

Russian lace eventually established itself as a local craft in a number of centres. A variety of articles of dress and household use were made of lace. Hand-made lace was produced in large quantities for the ornamentation of dowry sheets, towels, valances and apparel.

Russian peasant lace was most commonly of unbleached or white linen or cotton thread; coloured silks and gold and silver outlining threads were less frequently used; instead the patterns set against grounds were outlined with heavy raised or coloured threads of cotton or linen. The ornamentation was evidently inspired by embroidery and weaving, which were earlier types of Russian folk art.

The peasant laces of the eighteenth century are characterized by the linear treatment of the designs. These are mostly geometrical, and incorporate traditional motifs—plain and toothed diamonds, squares, triangles and meanders—basic elements which are combined into countless variations of repeating patterns.

Later, figurative subjects appear. Ancient symbolic motifs such as the peacock, a female figure (once a Goddess), the Tree of Life, and so on, were introduced into lace patterns during the second half of the eighteenth century, and became popular during the first half of the nineteenth century.

Also in use for the linen and furnishings of peasant households in the same period are formalized plant motifs such as floral wreaths, festoons, and scrolls of abstract and naturalistic foliage, sometimes resembling embroidered decoration.

Chief centres of peasant lace-production are known in seventeen provinces for the eighteenth and nineteenth centuries, but lace-making was widespread, with traditional patterns in each locality. The town of Galich in the Kostroma Province was one with fairly active industry, and a local style characterized by figural patterns incorporating fantastic and exotic animals (pls. 145, 146).

The advent of the Rococo style in the eighteenth century naturally influenced lace-making: a regular mesh was developed, and from the 1770s to the 1820s fashion demanded that the pattern become lighter and sparser. All the characteristics of Rococo, particularly its asymmetry, were exploited in Galich lace to great advantage (pls. 139–141).

The succeeding neoclassical influence produced a style of lace with a wide expanse of mesh ground and a scattering of medallions, plant and animal motifs (pls. 145–149). Silk thread was widely used, and the colourings became lighter and more delicate.

Towards the end of the eighteenth century some districts in the Vologda Province were emerging as centres of lace-making. Their lace employed ancient traditional motifs, and was especially rich in floral ornamentation. Patterns formed by a continuous line of tape lace were worked in white linen thread and joined by a net ground or by brides. A coloured silk thread often ran through the otherwise white twists of the vermiculated design. In the late eighteenth and early nineteenth centuries coloured silks and metal thread were used for the mesh ground or ornamental fillings only, creating rhythmical effects. A wedding-sheet offers a perfect example of this type of lace (pl. 151). Towards the mid-nineteenth century, lace-work using several colours gradually ceased.

Portrait of Tolstaya, *née* Lopukhina

Lace from Yelets in the Orel Province rapidly achieved prominence in the mid-nineteenth century by virtue of the fine quality of its linen thread and the skill of its worksmanship. One type had predominantly floral motifs with a great variety of ornamental fillings, and outlining thread, usually somewhat shiny, round the design on a fine net ground. Another type was an imitation of Valenciennes lace, and lacked the heavier thread. It was soft and delicate, and a favourite trimming for personal linen and fine muslin, particularly because it was easily laundered. The ground and pattern were worked at the same time, and although the floral patterns seemed modest, the lace was not inexpensive because of the technique by which the fine threads in the solid parts of the pattern emerged to form the regular diamond-shaped mesh ground.

The town of Mtsensk in Orel Province was known as a lace-making centre by the eighteenth century. Pieces dating from the mid-nineteenth century onward have bold geometricized foliage patterns of thick white or unbleached linen thread. The outlining of patterns with heavy cotton threads, coloured or white, provides an attractive contrast with the elaborate mesh grounds (pls. 171, 172).

No less attractive is the tape lace made in the town of Balakhna in the Nizhny Novgorod Province, the finest examples being produced in the first half of the nineteenth century (pls. 158, 159). Both the rich floral forms and the traditional motifs are ancient designs. The spaces between their raised outlines are filled with various grounds. Such lace of linen thread was characterized by its expert execution and balanced design. By contrast, delicate blonde lace of superb quality, made of the finest silk thread, was also produced there.

The lace industry of the Yaroslavl Province, centering upon Rostov the Great, produced in the first half of the nineteenth century tape lace with bold patterns of floral scrolls or schematized traditional motifs, contrasted with a ground mesh of *brides picotées* forming squares or diamonds (pls. 154, 156).

Vyatka lace made of raw linen thread, known from the eighteenth century, was developed widely in the nineteenth century. The patterns of this lace may incorporate figures or plant or geometrical motifs, the regular forms outlined with thick white cotton thread to contrast with the openness of the mesh ground (pl. 172).

The town of Kalyazin in the Tver Province is listed as a lace-making centre in the seventeenth century. In the eighteenth century the finest Mechlin lace was made there, its pattern outlined with a shiny thread on a hexagonal ground. By the first half of the nineteenth century, the town produced lace of unusually heavy linen thread in the tape lace technique, distinguished by the great density of its vermiculated design, created from narrow strips joined together (pl. 173).

Numerous simple designs worked from memory without a pricking were produced in the Mikhailov District of the Ryazan Province in the mid-nineteenth century (pls. 174, 175). Geometrical designs were composed of triangles, rectangles, zig-zags or wavy lines. They are distinguished by their close texture, and by the absence of any background mesh. The lace was made of heavy unbleached or white linen thread, with red or blue cotton thread added. Such lace was employed only for the insertions or trimmings of peasant homespun garments.

A new type of lace was introduced after the mid-nineteenth century, called Russian guipure lace. The traditional floral forms of guipure lace are joined by bar threads without any ground at all. In Russia new geometrical designs were developed, composed of large and small squares, small ovals, chevrons, wavy lines, diamond-shapes and brides. Sometimes the whole ornamentation consisted of an elaborate lattice of brides. Guipure lace was produced in Vologda, Yelets, Moscow and other lace-making centres (pls. 165, 167, 181). It was made with linen or white cotton thread, or with cream-coloured or black silks; in cheaper pieces, narrow strips of smooth black paper were used instead of black silk thread. An insertion of black thread (pl. 165) and a mat edge of white thread (pl. 167) are perfect examples of Russian guipure lace.

In the late nineteenth and early twentieth centuries, lace was lavished on fashionable dress—for ladies summer coats, dresses, blouses, scarves and jabots—as well as to adorn pillowcases, coverlets, table napkins and other articles of household use. A variety of different techniques was used, with local traditions sometimes falling into disuse and disappearing finally, sometimes disappearing from one area only to reappear in another lace-making centre. Eventually, lace-makers began to make whatever type of patterns urban fashion demanded, often entirely eclectic in style. Patterns, materials and loans to finance the lace-making were provided by lace dealers, upon whom lace-makers utterly depended, since their wages were meagre. Although, for instance, a lace veil might be sold for fifteen roubles in a shop, the Vologda lace-maker who had spent 320 hours in making it, working for sixteen hours a day, would earn no more than six roubles. Lace-makers were sometimes driven to make lace from coarser thread in less densely worked patterns, in order to produce more work in a given time. Yet the overall standard of Russian lace remained high enough to enable it to compete with the famous laces of European make.

Russian lace was first displayed at the 1873 World Fair in Vienna, where it won prizes. After this success, the demand for Russian lace grew rapidly, and soon Russia was exporting lace to Britain and the United States, to the Continent of Europe, and to the Middle East and China.

Russian lace-making, it will be apparent, has been flourishing for some three centuries, producing masterpieces at every stage of its development. Gold and silver laces of the late seventeenth and early eighteenth centuries are remarkable for their variety of design and their wealth of intricate shapes. Bobbin lace of the late eighteenth and early nineteenth centuries is particularly sophisticated in design, and expertly carried out. Even at the end of the nineteenth century, when lace-making by hand, along with other arts and crafts, suffered a relative decline, some exquisite specimens of lace were produced.

Modern Russian lace-makers turn for inspiration to gold and silver lace, or to the delicate perfection of the linen laces. They continue to show their work at international exhibitions, and often win the highest awards. They draw on local traditions and also innovate, enriching their craft with techniques, motifs and patterns of their own devising.

123 Detail of chalice-cover of gold and silver lace,
17th century

124 Gold lace on ecclesiastical vestment,
17th century

125   Edging of silver lace on phelonion,
      17th century

126 Chalice-cover edge of gold and silver lace,
17th century

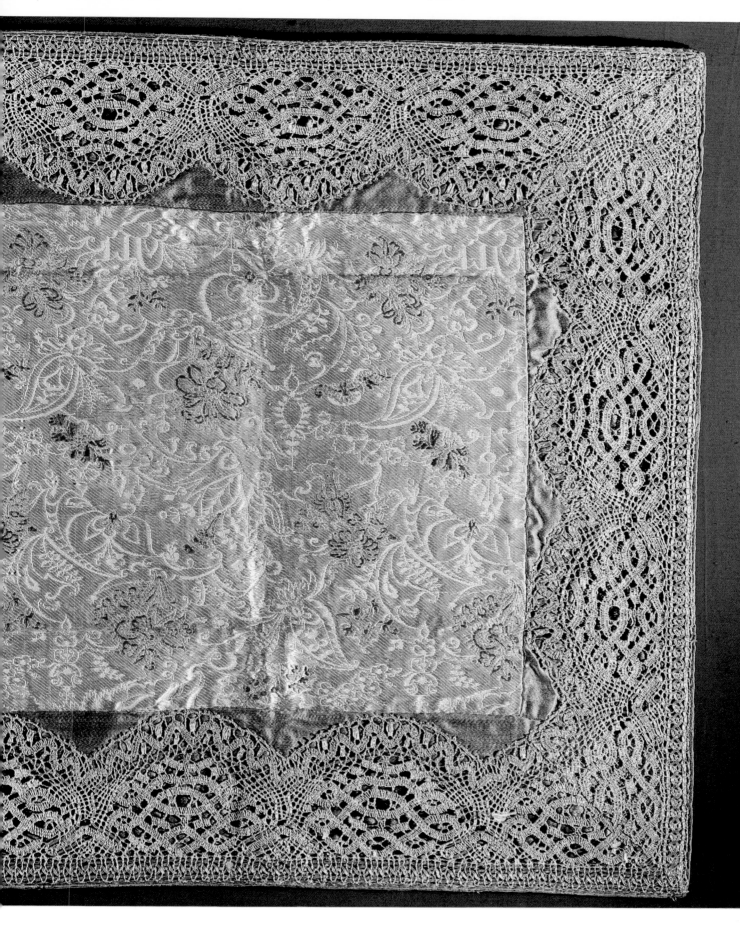

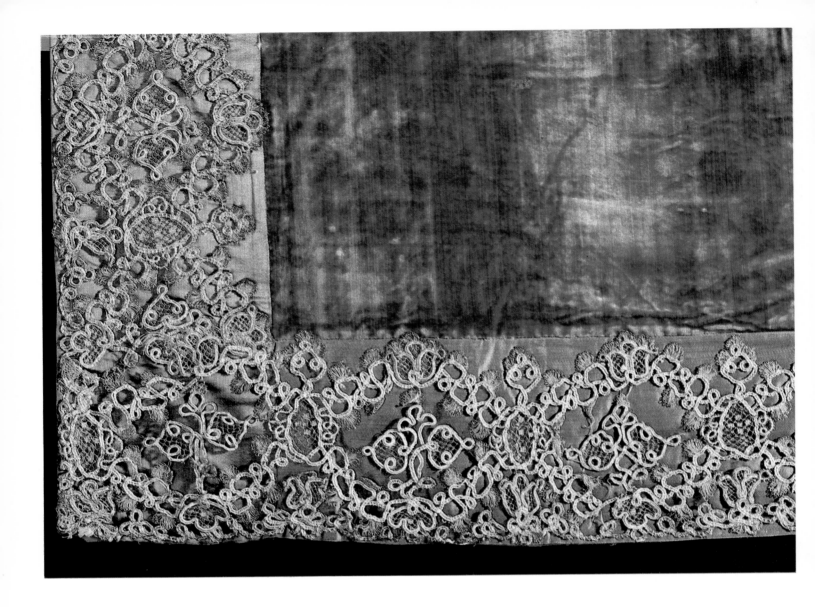

127   Shroud edge of gold and silver lace,
       first half of 18th century

128 Shroud edge of gold and silver lace,
mid-18th century

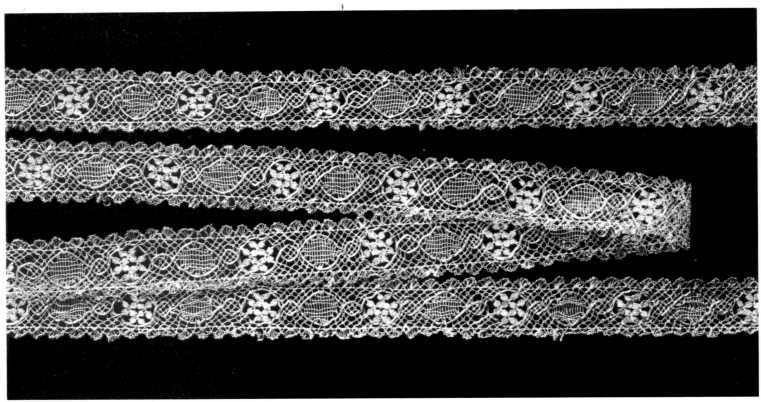

129 (Top) Chalice-cover edge of gold and silver lace, mid-18th century

130 (Above) Insertion of silver lace, 18th century

131   (Top) Galloon of gold lace.
       (Centre, above) Galloons of silver lace.
       18th century

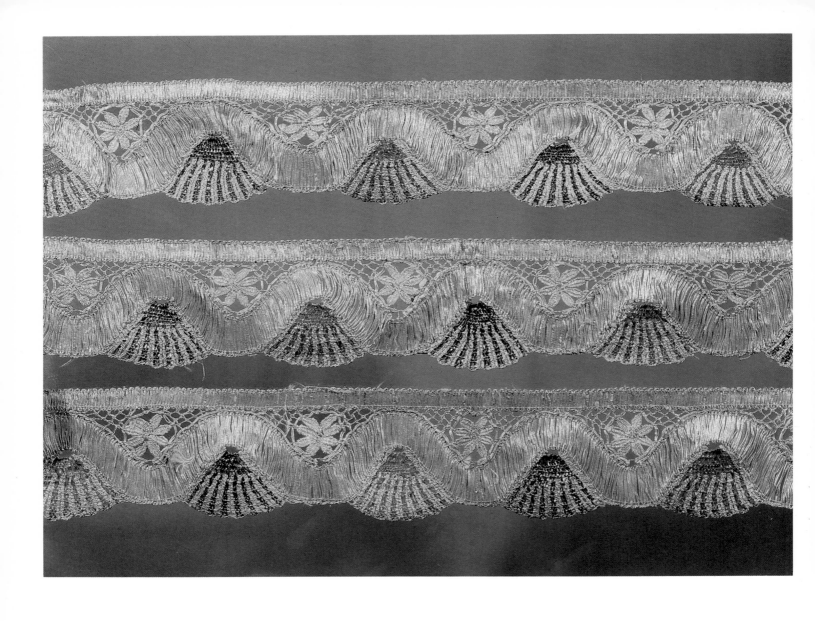

132 Edging of gold and silver lace,
second half of 18th century

133   Bed valance insertion of silver lace,
      late 18th century

134 Detail of scarf of silver lace,
mid-18th century

135 Towel edge of lace of coloured silks and gold thread,
      second half of 18th century

136   Detail of insertion of gold lace,
      late 18th or early 19th century

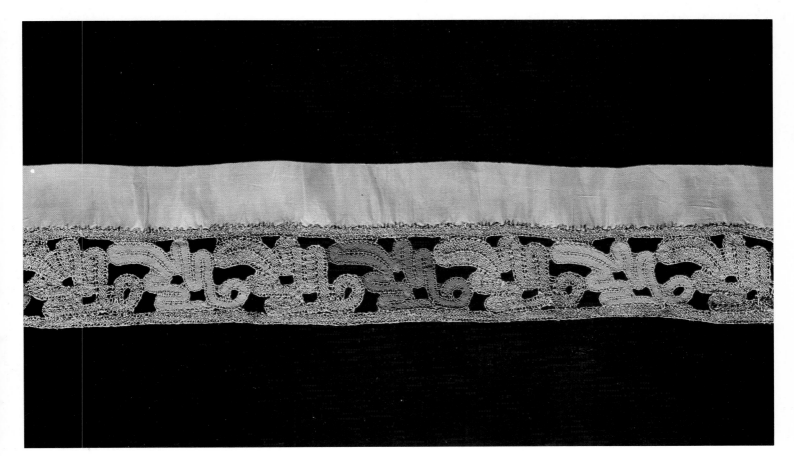

137 (Top) Towel edging of lace
     of silk and gold and silver thread,
     18th century

138 (Above) Detail of insertion
     of silks and gold thread,
     18th century

139 Detail of bed valance,
     Galich, Kostroma Province,
     late 18th century

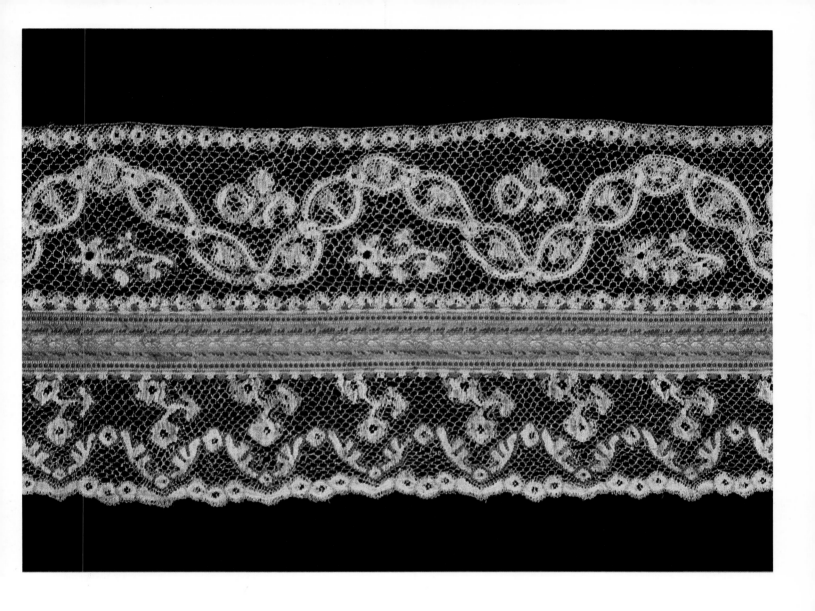

140 Detail of bed valance,
     Galich, Kostroma Province,
     late 18th century

141   Detail of bed valance,
      Galich, Kostroma Province,
      late 18th or early 19th century

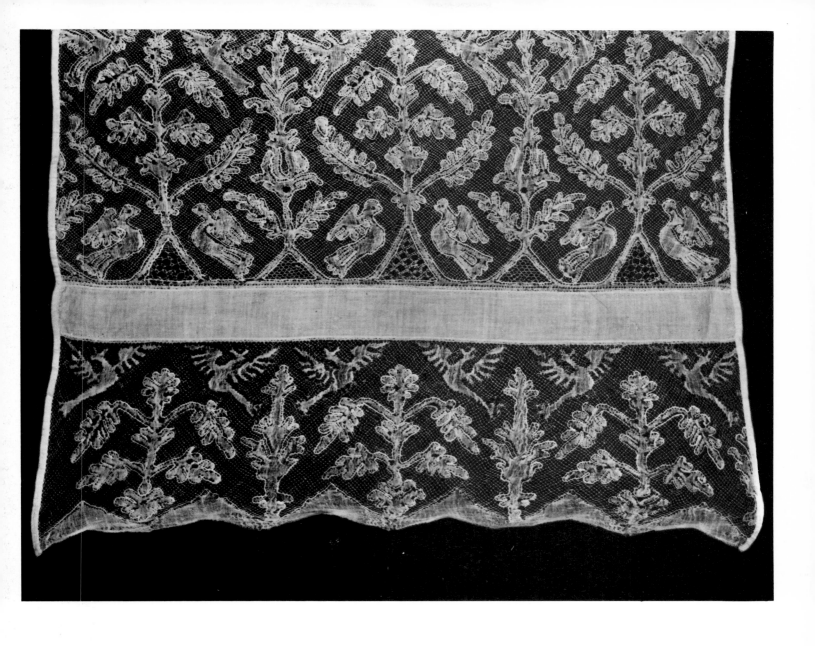

142 Detail of towel edge, Galich,
Kostroma Province,
late 18th or early 19th century

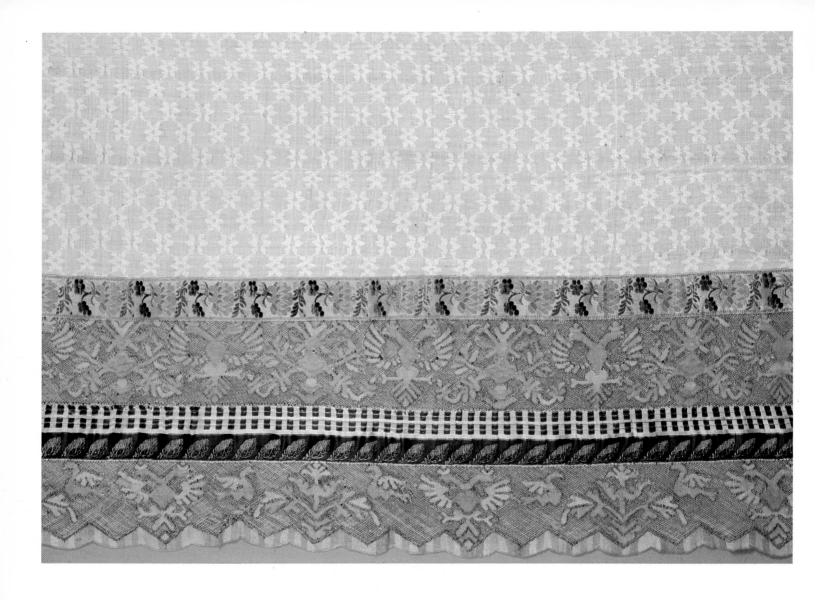

143 Towel edge,
Galich, Kostroma Province,
late 18th or early 19th century

144 Detail of bed valance,
    Galich, Kostroma Province,
    early 19th century

145 (Top) Detail of bed valance,
Galich, Kostroma Province,
early 19th century

146 (Above) Detail of bed valance,
Galich, Kostroma Province,
early 19th century

147   Detail of bed valance,
       Galich, Kostroma Province,
       early 19th century

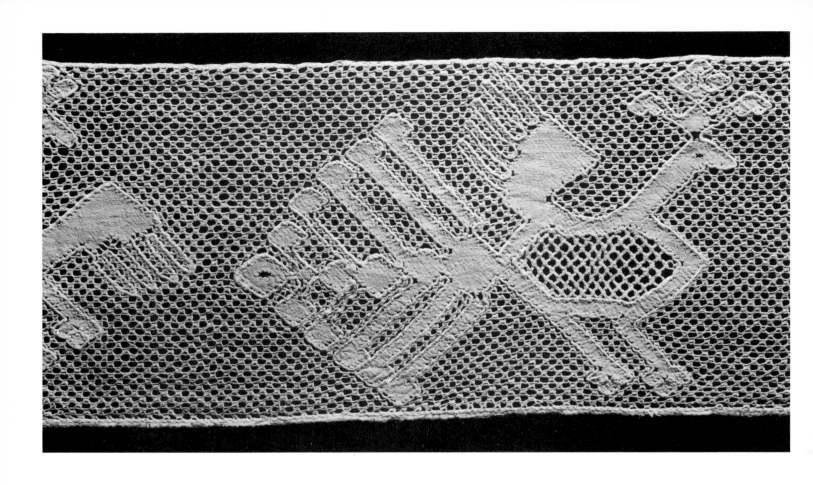

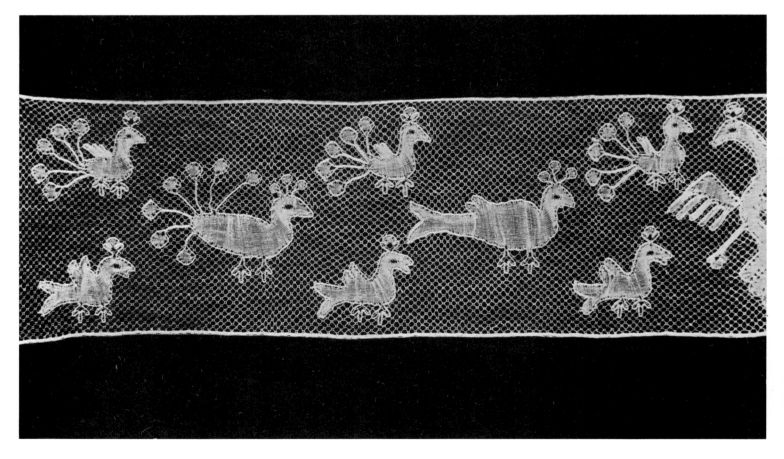

148 (Top) Detail of insertion,
Galich, Kostroma Province,
19th century

149 (Above) Detail of insertion,
19th century

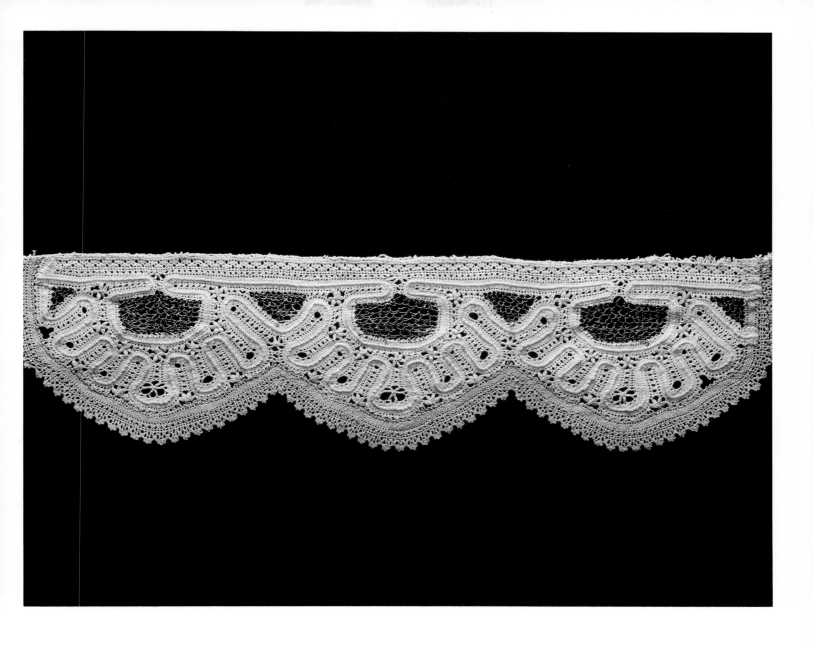

150 Towel edging of linen and silver lace,
Vologda Province,
first half of 19th century

151 Detail of wedding-sheet valance of silk and linen lace with gold thread insertion,
Vologda Province,
late 18th century

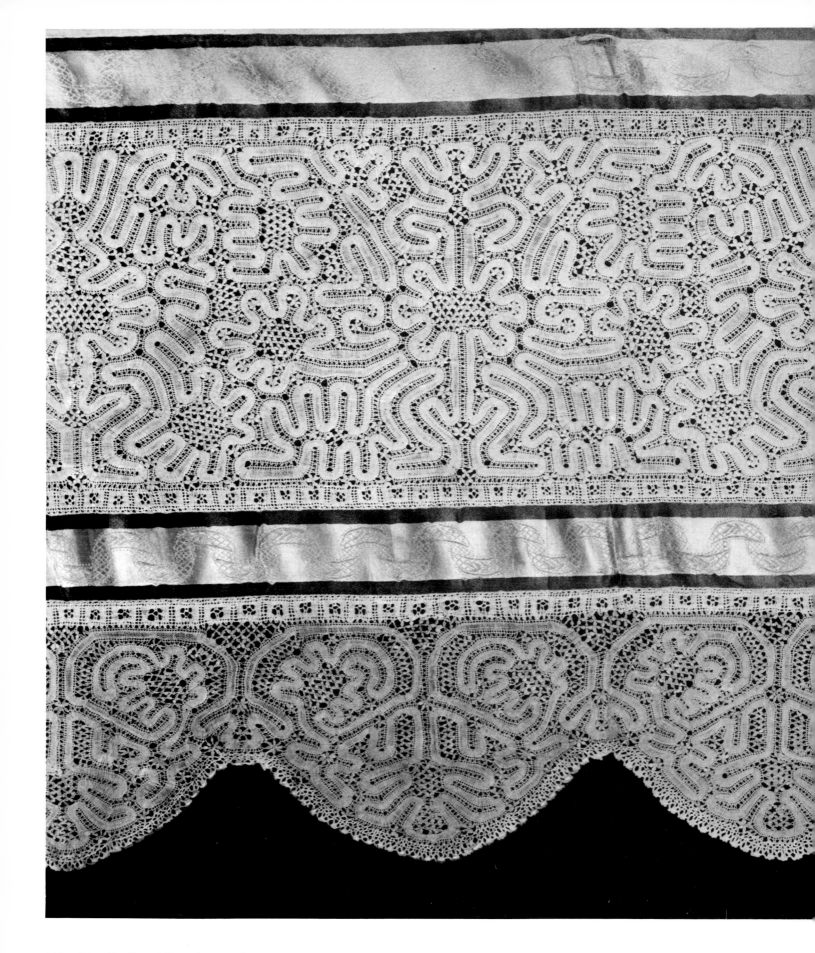

152 Detail of wedding-sheet valance,
Vologda Province,
late 18th or early 19th century

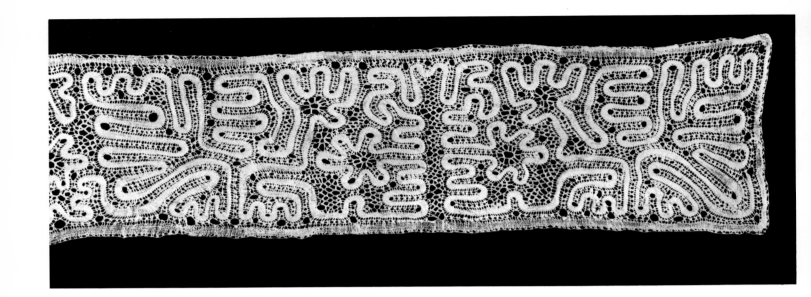

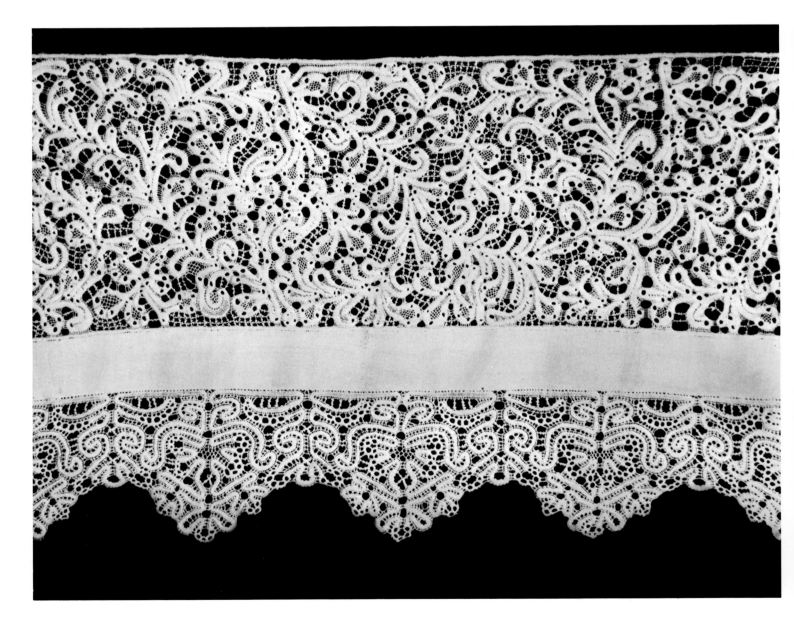

153 (Top) Detail of insertion,
Vologda Province,
first half of 19th century

154 (Above) Detail of sheet valance,
Yaroslavl Province,
second half of 18th century

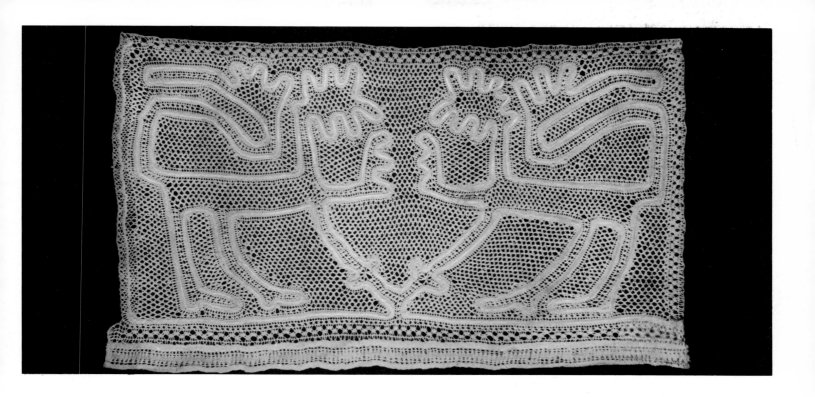

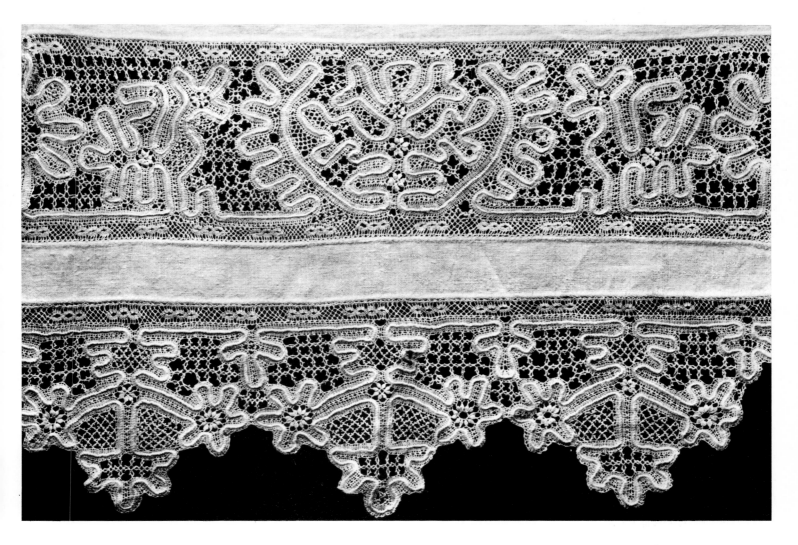

155 (Top) Insertion,
Vologda Province,
first half of 19th century

156 (Above) Detail of towel edging,
Rostov the Great, Yaroslavl Province,
first half of 19th century

157 Detail of sheet valance,
Vologda Province,
first half of 19th century

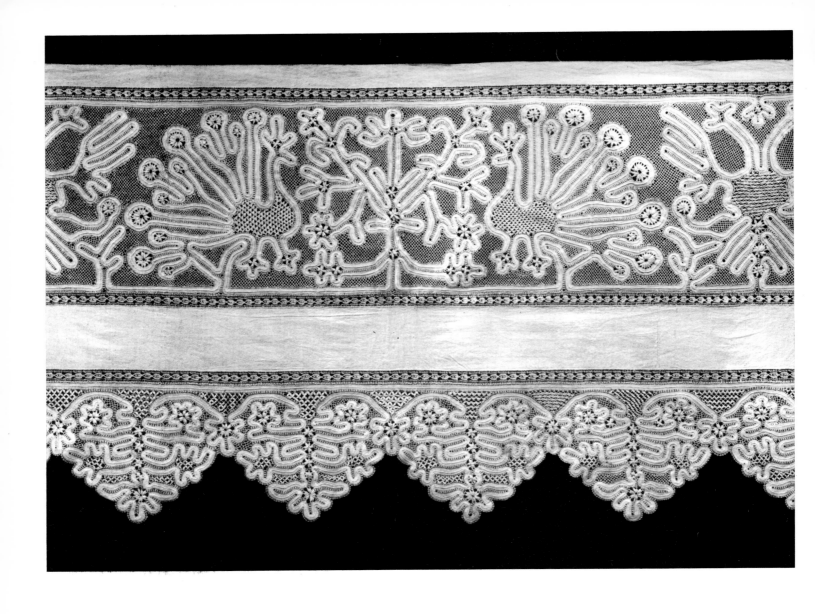

158 Detail of sheet valance (cf. Detail of lace, p. 148),
     Nizhny Novgorod Province,
     first half of 19th century

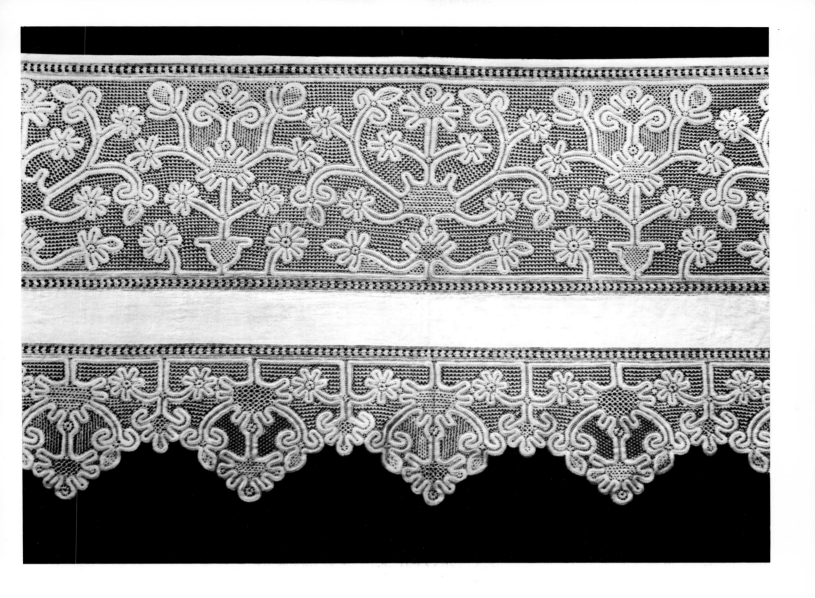

159   Detail of sheet valance,
Nizhny Novgorod Province,
first half of 19th century

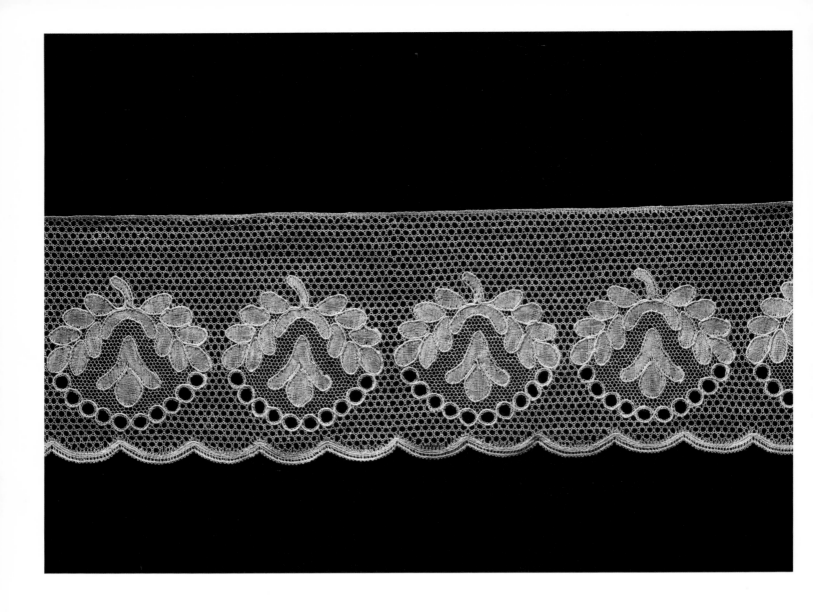

160 Detail of edging,
     Yelets, Orel Province,
     19th century

161 Detail of edging,
Yelets, Orel Province,
second half of 19th century

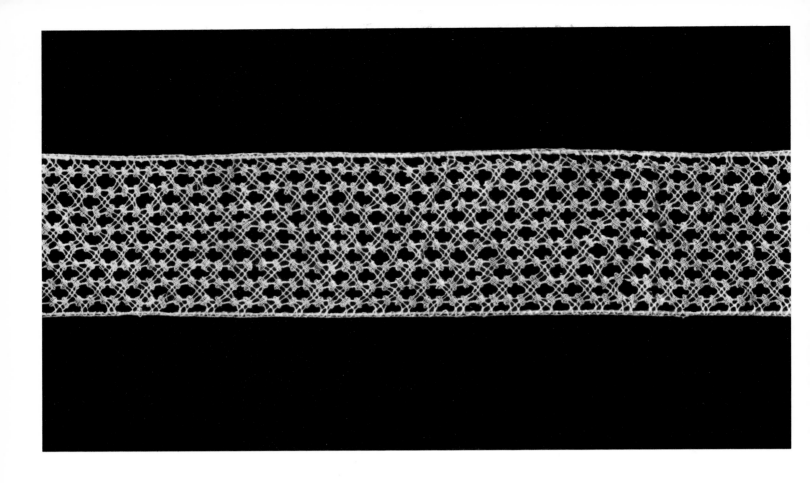

162 (Top) Detail of insertion,
Yelets, Orel Province,
19th century

163 (Above) Detail of edging,
Yelets, Orel Province,
mid-19th century

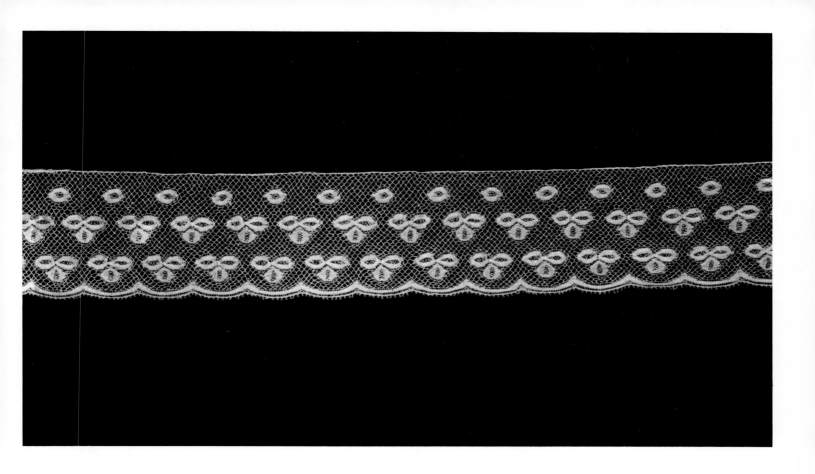

164 (Top) Detail of edging,
     Yelets, Orel Province,
     19th century

165 (Above) Detail of insertion,
     Yelets, Orel Province,
     early 20th century

166 Handkerchief border,
Yelets, Orel Province,
late 19th century

167 Mat border,
Yelets, Orel Province,
late 19th or early 20th century

168–9   Coverlet corner (above) and centrepiece (opposite),
Yelets, Orel Province,
late 19th century

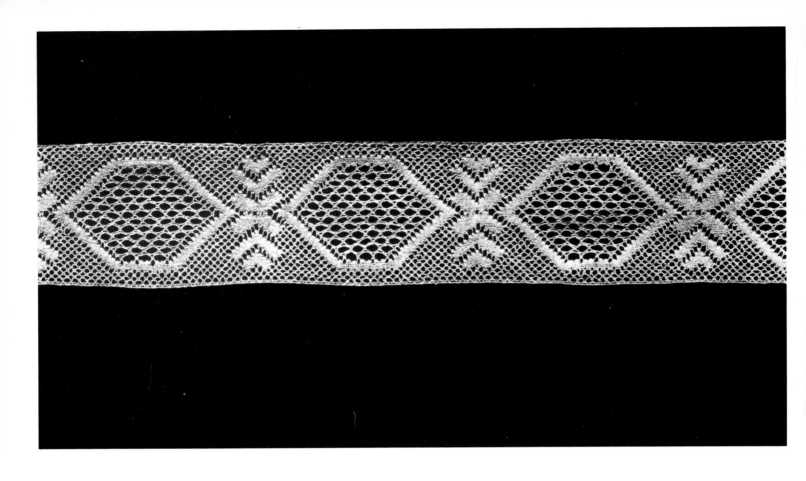

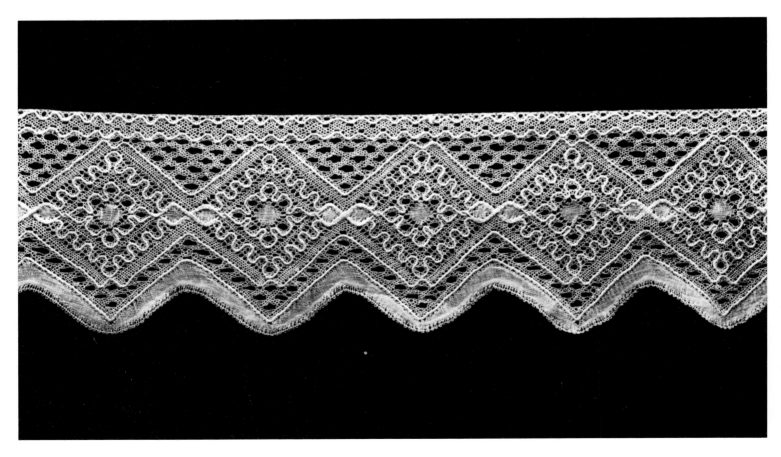

170 (Top) Detail of insertion,
 Mtsensk, Orel Province,
 late 19th or early 20th century

171 (Above) Detail of edging,
 Mtsensk, Orel Province,
 second half of 19th century

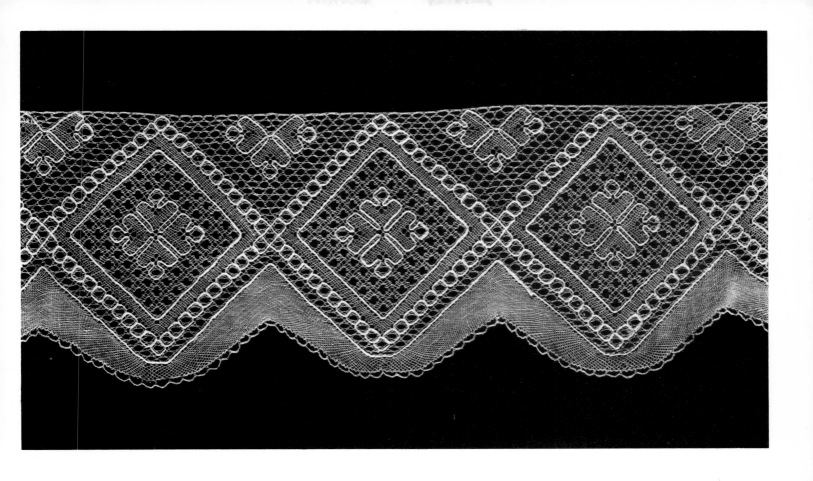

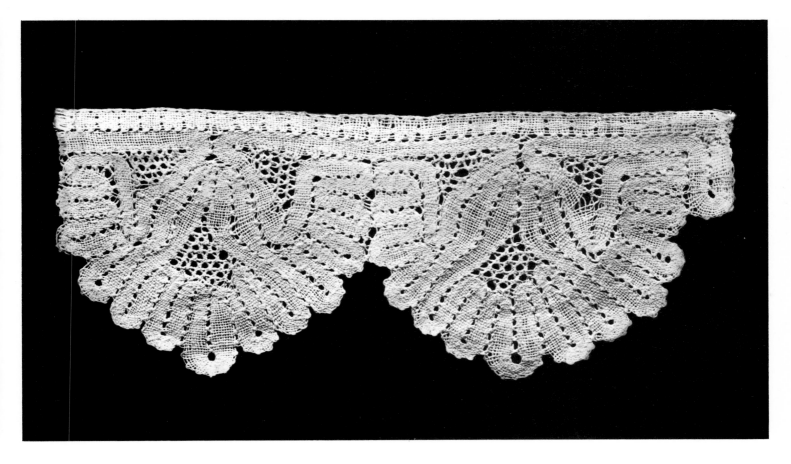

172 (Top) Detail of edging,
Vyatka Province,
late 19th century

173 (Above) Fragment of edging,
Kalyazin, Tver Province,
second half of 19th century

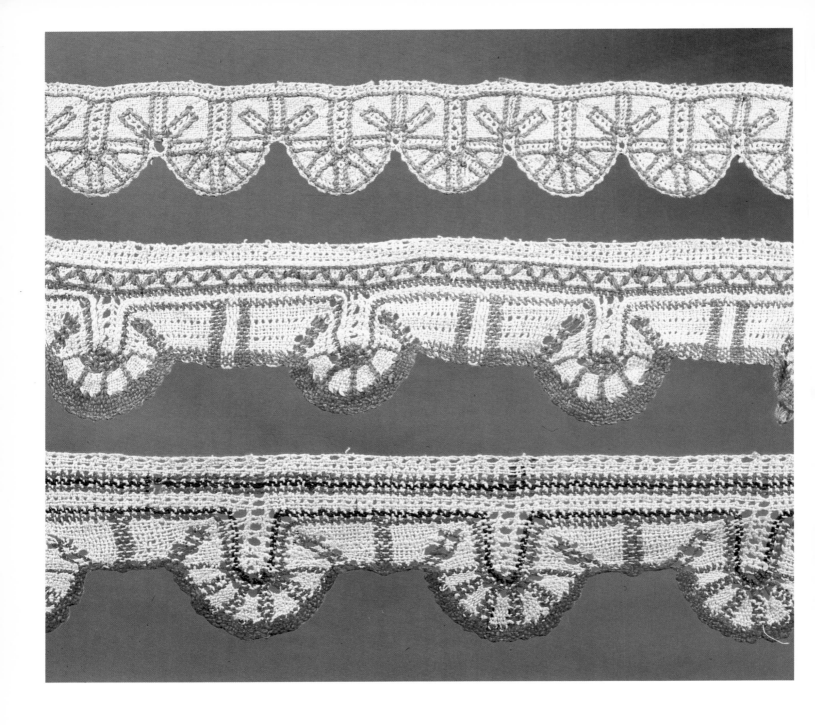

174   Details of edgings of peasant lace,
Mikhailov District, Ryazan Province,
19th century

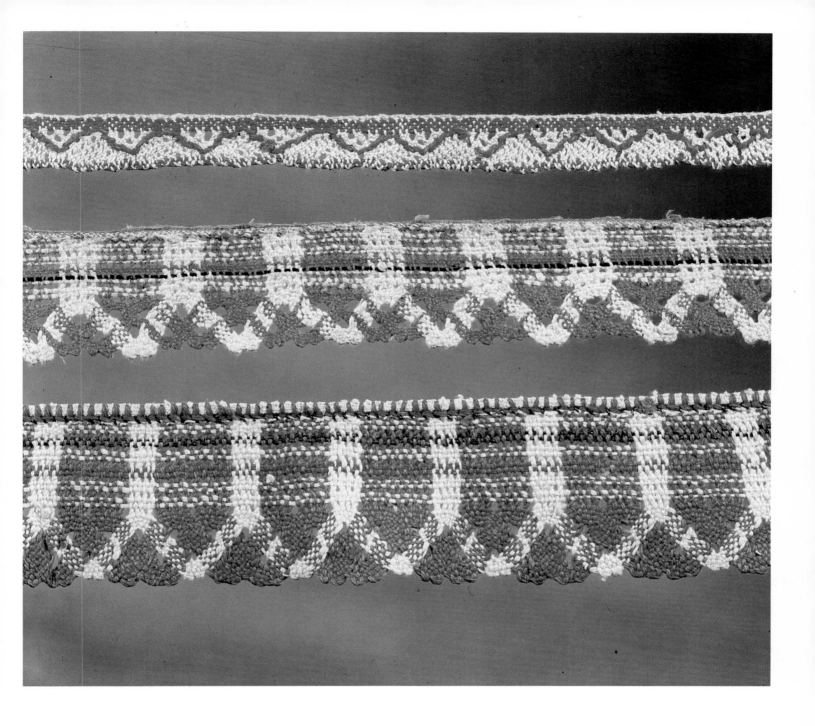

175 Details of edgings of peasant lace,
Mikhailov District, Ryazan Province,
19th century

176 (Top) Detail of insertion,
first quarter of 19th century

177 (Above) Detail of edging,
first quarter of the 19th century

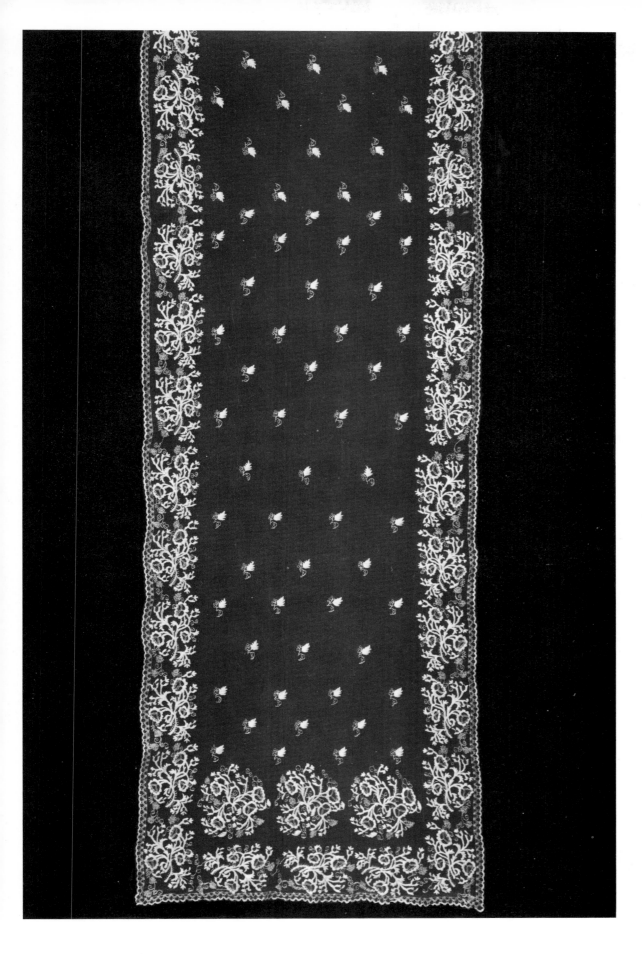

178 Detail of scarf,
    first half of 19th century

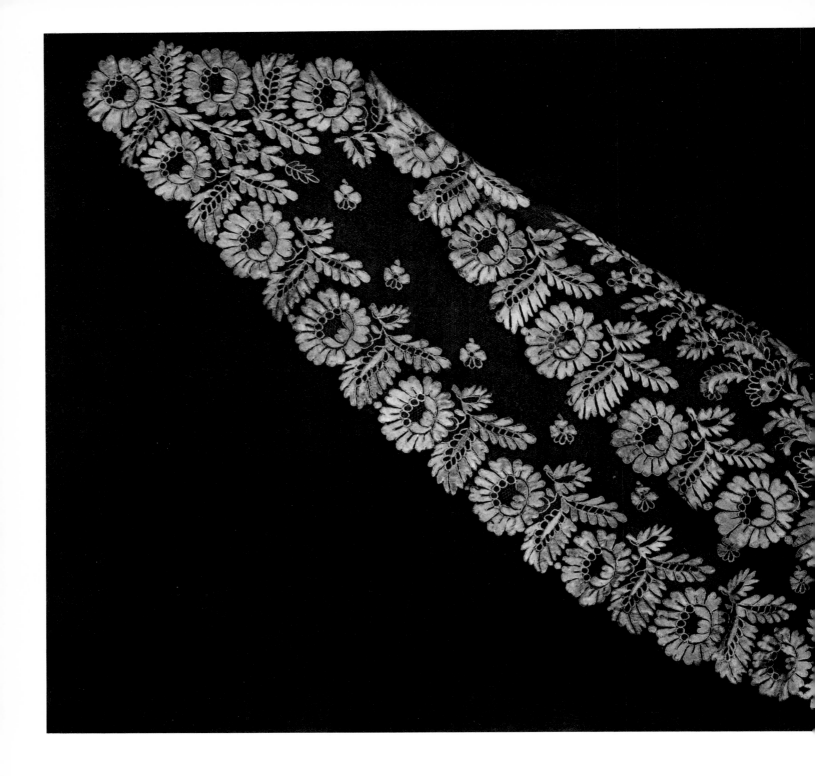

179   Shawl, 1820s

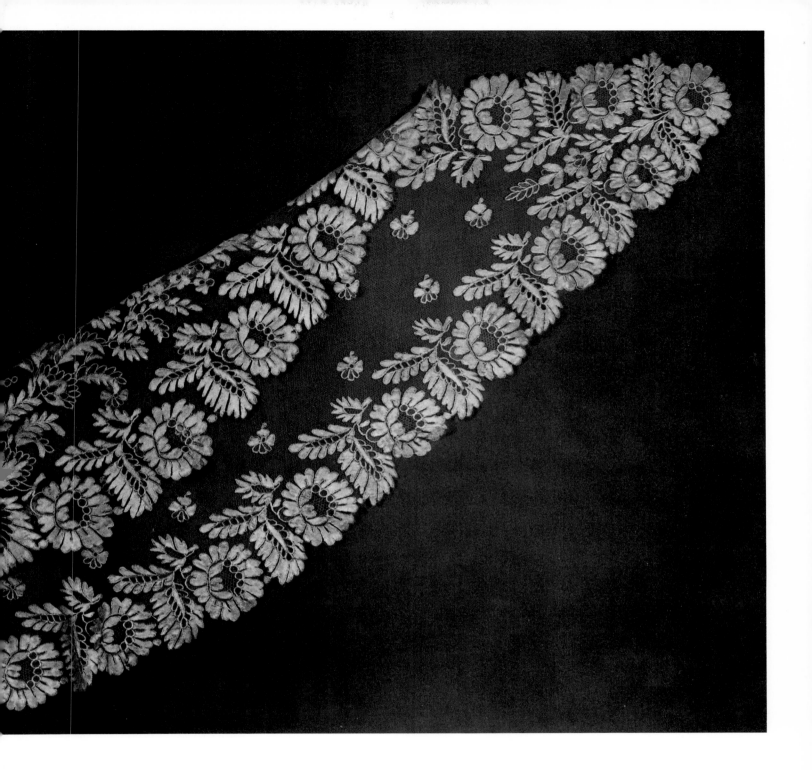

180 Detail of collar,
     mid-19th century

181 Trimming for neck of dress,
second half of 19th century

Notes on the Plates

Glossary

Index

Plates in the Text

The Embroidery

1   Altar frontal showing the Crucifixion with Interceding Saints
Novgorod, 12th century
Worked with couched gold and silver thread and silks in split-stitch on a silk ground
125 × 186 cm (49⅛ × 73⅛ in)
Acquired by the Museum in the 1920s
Acq. No. 55115 Р. Б.—1674

At either side of the Crucifixion are represented the Virgin Mary with Mary Magdalen (?), and St John with the Centurion Longinus. At the foot of the Cross is a cave with a skull. The eleven medallions in the border contain half-figures of Apostles, Christ and the Virgin Mary. A unique early Russian embroidery, this piece is worked in couched gold and silver thread, with the faces and hands embroidered with silks in a fine split-stitch. The figures are cut from the original ground of patterned polychrome twilled silk and applied on to a large-patterned piece of Byzantine silk. Several medallions have been lost.

2   Altar frontal with the Vernicle and Interceding Saints
Moscow, 1389
Worked with couched gold and silver thread and coloured silks in a fine split-stitch on a silk ground
123 × 221 cm (48⅜ × 87 in)
Acquired from the P. Shchukin Collection in 1906
Acq. No. 15494 Р.Б.—1

The composition depicts the Vernicle (the face of Christ on the veil of St Veronica), the Virgin Mary and St John, the Archangels Michael and Gabriel, and four Metropolitans of Moscow. In the lower register are placed eight busts of the Princes Vladimir, Boris and Gleb, Alexis the Man of God, Nicetas the Martyr, St Gregory The Divine and other saints. The border is occupied by half-figures of Angels, and has the four Evangelists in the corners. According to the inscription, the altar frontal was worked at the order of the Princess Maria, daughter of Prince Alexander Mikhailovich of Tver and wife of Semyon the Proud.

3–5   Altar frontal, known as the Suzdalian Shroud, showing the Communion of the Apostles
Moscow, between 1410 and 1423
Worked with coloured silks in a fine split-stitch and with couched gold and silver thread on a taffeta ground
114 × 210 cm (44⅞ × 22⅝ in)
Acquired from the P. Shchukin Collection in 1905–6
Acq. No. 19724 щ Р.Б.—2

Christ gives the Eucharist to the Apostles: to the left, the sharing of the consecrated bread; to the right, the sharing of the consecrated wine. Christ appears in an architectural setting against a background of scrolling stems. The centrepiece is enclosed within a gold-embroidered donor's inscription. The border shows scenes from the lives of the Virgin and Saints Joachim and Anna, and the corners have the four Evangelists.

6, 7   **Panel with the Deisis**
Moscow, late 15th or early 16th century
Worked with couched gold and silver thread and coloured silks in a fine satin stitch on a pale blue silk ground
11 × 64 cm (4¼ × 25⅛ in)
Acquired from the P. Shchukin Collection in 1905–6
Acq. No. 15974 щ Р.Б.—6I

The upper register of the panel with a nine-figure Deisis has round medallions and floral scrolls. The faces of the saints are depicted with highlights worked with modelling stitches; their features are slightly individualized. The work is distinguished by its restrained colouring and pictorial manner.

8   **Pall with figures of Prince Feodor of Yaroslavl and his sons David and Constantine**
Moscow, 1501
Worked with couched gold and silver thread and coloured silks in split-stitch on a silk ground
242 × 96 cm (95¼ × 37¾ in)
Acquired from the Rumiantsev Museum, Moscow, in 1914
Acq. No. 57779 Р.Б.—136

The composition is distinguished by its simple, rather severe treatment. Its restricted colour range is characteristic of the embroidered palls of the period. The inscription tells us that the pall was ordered in Moscow by Princess Maria, and was laid on Prince Feodor's coffin.

9   **Shroud showing the Assumption of the Virgin, known as 'The Cloudy Assumption'**
Sewing-rooms of Princess Staritsky, 1560s
Worked with couched gold and silver thread and coloured floss and twisted silks in a fine split-stitch; centrepiece of aubergine Italian damask, border of red damask
70 × 100 cm (27½ × 39⅜ in)
Acquired from the A. Uvarov Collection not later than 1917
Acq. No. 53116 Р.Б.—86

The death of the Virgin was an important theme in Byzantine painting. She is here surrounded by mourning Apostles and Angels, while Christ carries her soul (a child) in His arms. The border is embroidered with words of a hymn, and the central inscription identifies the shroud as a gift from the Staritsky family to the Monastery of St Cyril of Byelozersk. The pall is known as 'The Cloudy Assumption' because the Apostles are represented floating on clouds.

10   Icon of St Sophia, Divine Wisdom
     Moscow, early 16th century
     Worked with couched gold and silver thread and coloured silks in satin stitch on a ground of Italian
     damask
     41 × 39 cm (16⅛ × 15¼ in)
     Acquired from the A. Olsufyev Collection in 1891
     Acq. No. 23227 Р.Б.—190

The winged figure of St Sophia enthroned is flanked by the Virgin and St John the Baptist. Christ is represented above in a mandorla. The upper register of the icon contains the *hetimasia*, or preparation of the Throne for the Judgment. The colouring red of St Sophia's face and hands is the convention followed in contemporary icon painting.

11   Icon with figures of Saints Zosima and Savvaty
     Sewing-rooms of the Stroganovs, Solvychegodsk
     Second half of 17th century
     Worked with couched gold and silver thread and coloured silks in satin stitch on red satin
     34 × 27 cm (13⅜ × 10⅝ in)
     Acquired from the P. Shchukin Collection in 1905–7
     Acq. No. 15657 щ Р.Б.—10

The contours of the figures are outlined with a heavy gold thread, a characteristic feature of the embroideries of the Stroganovs' sewing-rooms. According to the inscription the icon was commissioned by Dmitry Stroganov.

12   Yoke of a phelonion
     15th century
     Worked with pearls, metal plaques and spangles on silk
     Length 43 cm (16⅞ in), width 76 cm (29⅞ in)
     Acquired in 1926; originally in the possession of Paphnutius, founder of a monastery near Kaluga (later
     the Monastery of St Paphnutius of Borovsk)
     Acq. No. 78291 Р.Б.—2664

The yoke is embellished with a scale-like ornament worked in pearls. Every almond-shaped scale is studded with a silver-gilt drop.

13   Panel
     Late 16th or early 17th century
     Worked with couched gold and silver thread on black velvet
     66.5 × 52 cm (25½ × 20½ in)
     Acquired from the P. Shchukin Collection in 1905–6
     Acq. No. 20305 щ Р.Б.—241

The repeated trefoil pattern contains such characteristic Sassanian motifs as confronted winged beasts, birds and panthers among formalized foliage scrolls. The composition is balanced, and the motifs are lively and vivid. Even the spaces of the field form intricate patterns. The panther with one forepaw raised is a protective beast.

14 Sleeve-band detail
Late 16th or early 17th century
Worked with couched gold and silver thread on red velvet
33 × 65 cm (13 × 25⅝ in), size of whole article
Acquired in 1929
Acq. No. 71787 Р.Б.—2359

The main repeat-motif of a Tree of Life is surrounded by lyre-like tulips and acanthus leaves arranged symmetrically, while the interstices contain unicorns and birds presented heraldically. The pattern glitters with gold and silver set against a red ground.

15 Detail of yoke of a phelonion
Late 16th or early 17th century
Worked with couched gold and silver thread on red velvet
Length 42 cm (16½ in), width 90 cm (35⅜ in), size of whole article
Acquired from the P. Shchukin Collection in 1905
Acq. No. 19941 щ Р. Б.—220

This truly superb embroidered work imitates the 'Gothic Rose' design characteristic of late 15th- and 16th-century Italian cut gold-brocaded velvet. In 17th-century records this embroidery technique is described as 'simulating velvet brocaded with gold loops'.

16 Panel
17th century
Worked with couched gold and silver thread and twisted coloured silks on black velvet
33 × 66.5 cm (13 × 26⅛ in)
Acquired from the P. Shchukin Collection in 1905
Acq. No. 19362 щ Р.Б.—206

The main repeat-motif is a falconry scene. Falcons grip their prey; smaller birds occupy floral scrolls. The border has a repeat bird motif enclosed within medallions, while the interstices contain a highly formalized floral pattern. A similar panel is described in the 17th-century inventory of the dowry of Princess Maria.

17 Detail of sleeve-band
17th century
Worked with couched gold and silver thread on red velvet
37 × 58 cm (14⅝ × 22¾ in), size of whole article
Acquired in 1927
Acq. No. 64149 В—3

The repeat-pattern is a Turkish-looking tulip, with acanthus leaves and a pomegranate, flanked by confronted gerfalcons seizing swans, presented heraldically. The stitching of details of leaves and sprays imitates Italian gold-brocaded velvet.
    The overall pattern contains motifs derived from both Oriental and Western fabrics. The folklore subject of a falcon attacking a swan was widely used in the decoration of 17th-century enamels of Solvychegodsk.

18   Panel

17th century
Worked with couched gold and silver thread on red velvet
34 × 66 cm (13³⁄₈ × 26 in)
Acquired in 1905
Acq. No. 19830 щ Р.Б.—209

The composition combines birds, crowned and collared with gold, and lush foliage and flowers. The elaborate pattern and refined technique illustrate the perfected skills of the embroiderers of Moscow sewing-rooms.

19   Panel

17th century
Worked with couched gold and silver thread on black velvet
35 × 70 cm (13³⁄₄ × 27¹⁄₂ in)
Acquired from the P. Shchukin Collection in 1905–6
Acq. No. 19869 щ Р.Б.—309

The pattern with medallions of Eastern origin arranged symmetrically, stylized flowers, winged horses, unicorns and long-necked birds presented heraldically, shows imperfections which suggest that the panel was worked by a peasant embroiderer imitating luxurious figured imported fabric, rather than by a professional embroiderer in a boyar sewing-room.

20   Panel

Second half of 17th century
Worked with couched silver and gold thread and with coloured silks on black velvet. The field is studded with gold spangles and many details are embroidered in raised work
34 × 66 cm (13³⁄₈ × 26 in)
Acquired from the P. Shchukin Collection in 1905
Acq. No. 19937 щ Р.Б.—327

In a composition characteristic of Russian embroidery in the 17th century, a central flower is enclosed in a floral circle and surrounded by interlacing stems and tendrils bearing blossoms, arranged symmetrically. The pattern is of Oriental origin. Vivid colours—silks of crimson, emerald green, yellow and blue—are enclosed by gleaming gold and silver thread.

21   Panel

Second half of 17th century
Worked with couched gold and silver thread and with coloured silks on black velvet
31 × 60 cm (12¹⁄₈ × 23⁵⁄₈ in)
Acquired in 1896 as part of 18th-century epitrachelion
Acq. No. 34115 Р.Б.—938

The central flower-motif is enclosed in a medallion of Sassanian derivation, surrounded by scrolling stems with blossoms and acanthus leaves. The pattern is close to contemporary designs of both Eastern and Western origin. The composition resembles the head-pieces in 17th-century Russian printed books.

22   Panel
Second half of 17th century
Worked with couched gold and silver thread on red velvet
33 × 68 cm (13 × 26¾ in)
Acquired from the P. Shchukin Collection in 1905
Acq. No. 19723 щ Р.Б.—245

The outlines of the pattern are reserved in plain velvet, and the rest of the panel is worked with gold and silver thread. This type of embroidery imitates Italian cut velvets brocaded with gold loops.

23   Yoke of a phelonion
Late 17th century
Appliqué of padded motifs embroidered with couched gold and silver thread. The red velvet ground is studded with gold spangles
Length 36 cm (14⅛ in), width 94 (37 in)
Acquired not later than 1917
Acq. No. 55753 В—4

An elaborate composition of stylized flowers, fruits and berries has the field covered all over with gold spangles. The raised elements were embroidered separately on birchbark or thick paper and sewn on to the ground. The ornamentation simulates the delicate filigree metalwork of the period. This technique is characteristic of needlework produced in the Tsarina's sewing-rooms in the late 17th and early 18th centuries.

24   Panel
Late 17th or early 18th century
Appliqué of padded motifs embroidered with gold and silver thread and twisted silks. The red velvet ground is studded with gold spangles
18 × 66.5 cm (7 × 25¾ in)
Acquired in 1905
Acq. No. 197 щ Р.Б.—339

At the centre of this highly dynamic composition is the Tree of Life motif with confronted lions. Fabulous birds and griffins presented in heraldic pairs occupy the interstices.

25   Woman's headdress
17th century
Worked with couched gold and silver thread and heavy bullion on scarlet silk
Height 19 cm (7½ in)
Acquired from the Rumiantsev Museum, Moscow, in 1923
Acq. No. 54722–380

Medallions and rosettes, and shells at the back, are embroidered with pearls. A type of peasant wedding headdress *(soroka)* which became popular in the 19th century is very similar to this 17th-century example.

26   Liturgical cuffs
Late 17th or early 18th century
Worked with pearls, gold cord, heavy bullion and spangles on red velvet
Length 25 cm (9¾ in), width 14 cm (5½ in)
Acquired in 1939
Acq. No. 81594 Р.Б.—4255

The scalloped embroidered decoration has a repeat pattern of tulips and foliate scrolls. Such decorative bands, either scalloped or plain, were usual on the edges of both rich clothing and ecclesiastical vestments of the period. More usually the scallops would face inward (cf. pls. 126–128).

27   Yoke of ecclesiastical vestment
Late 17th or early 18th century
Worked with pearls, precious stones and gold on red velvet
30 × 62 cm (11¾ × 24⅜ in)
Acquired in 1930
Acq. No. 68986 OK 1186

Floral design in Oriental style, with rectangular border. The pearls, emeralds and other precious stones create an effect of extreme luxury.

28   Yoke of ecclesiastical vestment (cf. pl. 26)
Late 17th or early 18th century
Worked with pearls, gold cord and spangles, gold studs, emeralds and rubies on black velvet
Length 40 cm (15⅝ in), width 65 cm (25⅝ in)
Acquired in 1939
Acq. No. 81594 Р.Б.—4225

The soft lustre of the seed pearls sets off the greater brightness of the large pearls, against a ground of gold spangles. The pattern is outlined with heavy gold cord for stronger definition. The embroidered flowers are inset with rubies and emeralds.

29   Man's shirt
17th century
Worked with gold and silver thread on a fine muslin ground in satin stitch and stem stitch
Length 81 cm (31⅞ in), width of hem 184 (72⅜ in)
Acquired from the Rumiantsev Museum, Moscow, in 1923
Acq. No. 54722–142

The neck-opening, upper sleeve and front slit are bordered with a light linear pattern of scrolls incorporating a lyre-like motif. Scarlet taffeta strips sewn along some of the seams enhance the decorative effect. Similar shirts are described in the 1624 inventory of the donations of the Tsar.

30   Ceremonial *shirinka* towel
17th century
Worked with coloured floss silks and silver thread in satin and running stitch on a muslin ground
55 × 55 cm (21⅝ × 21⅝ in)
Acquired in 1897
Acq. No. 34967 C—377

The border design is of floral scrolls with double palmettes in the corners, outlined with black thread. It resembles the linear painted decoration on distaffs from the Northern Dvina area. The long fringe is of silk and silver threads.

31   Ceremonial *shirinka* towel
17th century
Worked with gold and silver thread and coloured twisted silks in satin and stem stitch on a white silk ground
33 × 30 cm (13 × 11¾ in), original shape lost
Acquired in 1933
Acq. No. 75361 Р.Б.—2681

The pattern is made up of a wavy band with repeat interwined knots and lyre- and lily-motifs, outlined with black thread.

32   Fragment of ceremonial *shirinka* towel (?)
Late 17th or early 18th century
Worked with gold and silver thread and coloured floss silks in satin and stem stitch on fine linen
12 × 12.5 cm (4⅝ × 4⅞ in)
Acquired in 1927
Acq. No. 54722 B—38

The creature at the centre of the design is the Sirin, the bird with a woman's head, originally an auspicious creature. The same design appears in numerous works of decorative art.

33, 34   Details of gold-embroidered panel
First half of 18th century
Worked with couched gold thread and gold spangles on red velvet
16.5 × 16.5 cm (6½ × 6½ in), 17 × 17 cm (6⅝ × 6⅝ in)
Acquired from the P. Shchukin Collection between 1905 and 1911
Acq. No. 21285 щ 109, 110

The representation of foliage and birds is naturalistic; the inspiration very probably derives from Russian folk art.

35   Top of *kokoshnik* headdress
Moscow Province
Second half of 18th century
Worked with couched gold thread and coloured foil and spangles on red velvet
27 × 22 cm (19⅝ × 8⅝ in), oval
Acquired in 1952
Acq. No. 87848 Кр. б. 240

The Tree of Life motif is flanked by pairs of confronted birds. The stitches display a high degree of technical skill; the composition is balanced and the pattern harmonious.

36   Back of *kokoshnik* headdress
Central Russia
Second half of 18th century
Worked with couched gold and silver thread, metal strip and spangles on red velvet
Height 45 cm (17⅝ in), width of base 33 cm (13 in)
Acquired not later than 1917
Acq. No. 54786 Кр. б. 19

The central motif is a spray of flowers tied with a ribbon. The composition well suits the shape of the headdress. The stylized flowers can be identified as carnations, tulips and wild roses. The embroidery imitates embrossed metalwork of the period.

37   Back of *kokoshnik* headdress
Central Russia
Late 18th century
Worked with couched gold and silver thread on red velvet
Height 52.5 cm (20⅝ in), width of base 45 cm (17⅝ in)
Acquired in 1900
Acq. No. 38313 Кр. б. 53

The pattern is of a stylized vase with double carnations and other opulent flowers. The composition well suits the ogee-arch shape of the headdress. The pattern is outlined with fine raised stitches of silver thread which soften the effect of the gold.

38   Back of *kokoshnik* headdress
Central Russia
Second half of 18th century
Worked with couched gold and silver thread, spangles, heavy bullion and coloured foil on green velvet
Height 34 cm (13⅜ in), width of base 45 cm (17⅝ in)
Acquired from the P. Shchukin Collection in 1905–6
Acq. No. 23287 щ—9. Кр. б.

The amphora-shaped vase and stylized flowers of the pattern, almost sprawling across the ground, are decorated with zig-zags, tracery and chequers. The outlines are worked in fine raised stitches. An especially festive appearance is created by the use of coloured foil. The effect of the skilfully executed pattern is enhanced by the plain background areas of soft, lustrous velvet.

39 *Kokoshnik* headdress
Moscow Province
Early 20th century
Worked with couched spun gold thread and spangles on crimson velvet
Height 19 cm (7½ in)
Acquired not later than 1917
Acq. No. 54786–236

The central motif is a bunch of carnations tied with a bow. A chain motif runs round the lower edge. The linear pattern is widely spaced out over the surface. The impression is of breadth and splendour, enhanced by the exquisite colouring.

40 Fragment of a cloak
Second half of 18th century
Worked with couched gold thread and gold strip, heavy bullion and coloured foil strip on red velvet
Length 78 cm (30⅝ in), width 26 cm (10⅛ in)
Acquired not later than 1917
Acq. No. 56512 Б—628

The symmetrical pattern is of carnations, wild roses and pomegranates, motifs of Oriental derivation. The flower-heads etc. are filled with gold tracery and coloured foil strips. The pattern is outlined in fine raised stitches, so lightening the solid shapes of the flowers. A *yepancha* cloak was a peasant woman's garment, usually worn over a *sarafan* (pl. 120). It was a short, circular mantle of velvet, silk or brocade, suspended from shoulder-straps.
     This fragment has been used to form the crescent-shaped front of a *kokoshnik* headdress.

41 Two purses and (centre) a reticule
Late 18th or early 19th century
Worked with couched gold and silver thread and spangles on velvet
12 × 11 cm (4⅝ × 4¼ in); 10 × 7 cm (3⅞ × 2⅝ in); 14 × 17 cm (5½ × 6⅝ in)
Acquired from the P. Shchukin Collection in 1905–6
Acq. Nos. 22757 щ В—1224, 22895 щ В—1287, 22931 щ В—1212

Purse-making was an important branch of domestic needlework. Small bags, knitted, netted or worked in buttonhole stitch over moulds of wood or metal, were in continual demand for both men and women. Metal frames and fastenings were extremely costly, and for most people unobtainable. In the absence of metal fastenings, purses were drawn up with cords which also had to be made in the home.
     The patterns and manner of execution of the purses to the right and left are characteristic of peasant embroidery. The ornamentation of the reticule shows urban influence.

42 Sleeve of woman's blouse
Tver Province, northern Russia
Late 18th or early 19th century
Worked with gold thread in couched and raised work on crimson velvet
Length 65 cm (25½ in), width 39 (15¼ in)

Acquired from the N. Shabelskaya Collection in 1892
Acq. No. 22858 Б—1003

The dominant motif is a vase or pot holding highly stylized flowers and bunches of grapes, with confronted birds. Above and below are bands of squares containing geometrical rosettes. The band-pattern resembles the decoration on peasant towels and bed valances.

43   Back of woman's jacket
Nizhny Novgorod Province, southern Russia
Late 18th or early 19th century
Worked with gold and silver thread on couched and raised work on red velvet
Length 60 cm (23⅝ in), width hem 168 cm (66⅛ in)
Acquired in 1909
Acq. No. 45837–3

Flowers, grapes and occasional bows are filled in network, or have satin stitch. The *dushegreya* jacket, a short-waisted woman's garment, has a peplum of cylindrical folds. It was worn on festive days by well-to-do peasants or townswomen.

44   Back of *kokoshnik* headdress
Olonetsk Province, northern Russia
Late 18th or early 19th century
Worked with couched gold thread, gold cord and faceted glass beads on velvet
Height 24 cm (9⅜ in), width base 15 cm (5⅞ in)
Acquired in 1897
Acq. No. 34643–116

The piece is worked with a large overall pattern, each element being outlined with a thick gold cord. The centre of this highly formalized composition is occupied by a fantastic tree, its curved branches forming medallions and scrolls. The ornament includes birds, beasts, and the traditional horse and rider and female figure. Much of the decoration has symbolic significance. The female figure is probably a spinning-woman, and was once a deity. Similar motifs, though not typical in peasant embroidery, were widely popular in paintings on wooden distaffs in the northern Dvina area.

45   Back of *kokoshnik* headdress
Late 18th or early 19th century
Worked with couched gold and silver thread on red velvet
Length 23.5 cm (9⅛ in), width base 17.5 cm (6⅞ in)
Acquired in 1927
Acq. No. 61884–1134

The decorated area is covered with gold and silver tracery. The central figure, a female dancer, is encircled by birds, beasts and flowers of intricate design. It is possible to recognize a pair of ram's horns, confronted Sirin-birds, and griffins.

46 *Kokoshnik* headdress
Central Russia
Late 18th or early 19th century
Worked with mother-of-pearl beads, faceted glass beads, metal studs and spangles on a silver foil ground
Height 32 cm (12⅝ in), width base 38 cm (15 in)
Acquired in 1896
Acq. No. 34291–28

The stylized pattern is based on three large flowers with interlacing stems and foliage.

47 *Kokoshnik* headdress
Toropets District, Pskov Province, northern Russia
Late 18th or early 19th century
Worked with lace and seed pearls
Height 23 cm (9 in)
Acquired from the P. Shchukin Collection in 1905
Acq. No. 23151 щ. Кр. б. 190

The top of the headdress is a pointed arch made of figured silk. The insertion has raised cones symbolizing fertility, set against a background worked all over in seed pearls. There is also a mesh-like fringe of seed pearls. Such headdresses were worn only by well-to-do peasants or townswomen. An even more elaborate example of the same type of headdress is worn by the woman depicted in the painting illustrated on page 15.

48 Headdress of unmarried peasant girl
Vologda Province, northern Russia
Early 19th century
Worked with couched gold thread on silk, and with seed pearls and mother-of-pearl beads on a foil ground
Height 14 cm (5½ in), without festoons
Acquired from the P. Shchukin Collection in 1905–6
Acq. No. 16173 щ—629

Floral tracery decorates the band. The scalloped edge is made of triple festoons of seed pearls. The back has broad streamers of silk, embroidered with a floral motif of couched gold. The openwork pearl decoration gives a festive appearance to the headdress, which was usually worn when a girl was bethrothed.

49 Woman's headdresses
Rzhev District, Tver Province, northern Russia
Late 18th or early 19th century
Worked with seed pearls, gold spangles and coloured faceted glass beads on velvet
Height 16 cm (6¼ in), 9 cm (3½ in), 9 cm (3½ in)
Acquired from the P. Shchukin Collection in 1905–6
Acq. Nos. 23289 щ. Кр. б. 205, 23301 щ. Кр. б. 208, 54786. Кр. б. 202

Formalized plant motifs are outlined with a heavier gold cord. These headdresses in the shape of inverted flower-pots were usually embellished with pearl-decorated nets which covered the head. We see such a headdress worn by a young woman in a portrait illustrated on page 19.

50   Shawl border
      Nizhny Novgorod Province, southern Russia
      19th century
      Worked with couched gold and silver thread, metal strip and heavy bullion on black satin
      69 × 146 cm (27 1/8 × 57 1/2 in)
      Acquired from the Bakhrushin Collection in 1904
      Acq. No. 42567 Д—603

Naturalistic floral and foliate motifs are fancifully entwined to give the impression of intricate scrollwork. There is an outer border of formalized leaves separated by scrolls.

51   Shawl
      Nizhny Novgorod Province, southern Russia
      Late 18th or early 19th century
      Worked with couched gold thread and metal strip, heavy gold and silver bullion and spangles on dark blue taffeta. There is a short fringe of gold threads
      98 × 97 cm (38 5/8 × 38 in)
      Acquired from the P. Uvarova Collection in 1922
      Acq. No. 53977 Д—63

Cascading over the surface from the corner vases are flowers, bunches of grapes and pomegranates. The gold threads with metal strip and bullion create a three-dimensional effect of light and shade.

52   Corner of shawl
      Kargopol District, Olonetsk Province, northern Russia, 1882
      Worked with couched gold thread on coarse white calico
      105 × 104 cm (41 1/4 × 41 in)
      Acquired by the Museum expedition to the Kargopol Region in 1950
      Acq. No. 83206 Д—854

From a solar rosette radiates a geometrical foliate design. The two side-corners are embroidered with formalized branches and blossoms. The embroiderer has set her name and the date on either side of the pattern as if continuing the narrow ornamental border.

53   Corner of shawl
      Kargopol District, Olonetsk Province, northern Russia, 1900s
      Worked with couched gold and flat-sided metal threads on coarse white calico. Two sides are trimmed with a dense fringe of twisted gold wire
      107 × 105 cm (42 × 41 1/4 in), size of whole article
      Acquired by the Museum expedition to the Kargopol region in 1950
      Acq. No. 83206 Д–853

Although the design of medallions, small flowers and carnations is worked in heavy metal thread, it seems light and graceful due to the open arrangement of the elements of the composition.

54 Detail of bed valance
Kostroma Province, southern Russia
Late 18th or early 19th century
Drawn threadwork with linen and coloured silks; edging of bobbin lace
Length 160 cm (63 in), width 40 cm (15⅝ in), size of whole article
Acquired in 1927
Acq. No. 61432 3–791

The centre of the repeat pattern is a double-headed eagle, flanked by birds, a tree, a couple and horse and rider. The detail is sufficient to show the traditional garments worn by Russian peasant women.

55 Towel edge
Galich, Kostroma Province, southern Russia
Early 19th century
Drawn threadwork with linen and coloured silks; edging of bobbin lace
Length 45 cm (17⅝ in), width 28 cm (11 in)
Acquired in 1892
Acq. No. 26965–885

The traditional subjects of symmetrically arranged female figures and horse-and-rider flanking the Tree of Life are treated naturalistically.

56 Detail of bed valance
Tver Province, northern Russia
18th century
Drawn threadwork with linen and coloured silks; edging of bobbin lace
Length 290 cm (114 in), width 150 cm (59 in), size of whole sheet
Acquired not later than 1917
Acq. No. 59690–9

The repeat pattern incorporates a lyre-like motif (perhaps an extremely conventionalized Tree of Life) flanked by unicorns presented heraldically. Small lozenges, saltire crosses and rosettes are scattered on the ground. The figural panel is bordered by bands with geometricized foliage motifs. The sheet was probably a wedding gift or part of a bride's dowry; the unicorn was a symbol of purity.

57 Bed valance
Archangel Province(?), northern Russia
18th century
Whitework embroidery with linen thread and drawn threadwork on a linen ground

Length 83 cm (32⅝ in), width 31 cm (12⅛ in)
Acquired from the I. Bilibin Collection in 1922
Acq. No. 54025–173

The pattern arranged with an axial symmetry is a central rosette surrounded by scrolling stems and flowers. The border on three sides is patterned with a continuous waving stem carrying floral scrolls. The ornamental fillings skilfully worked with glossy linen thread are conventional geometrical motifs—lozenges, saltire crosses, zig-zags, nettings and the like—known in Slav art from time immemorial. The ornamentation is inspired by the traditional motifs of Russian gold embroidery, as well as incorporating motifs popular in 17th-century decorative and applied arts.

58   Bed valance
Late 18th or early 19th century
Drawn threadwork with linen thread; edging of bobbin lace
Length 230 cm (90½ in), width 82 cm (32¼ in)
Acquired in 1896
Acq. No. 34024–130

The design contains a formalized river scene, and it is suggested that the composition represents a festival on the Neva in St Petersburg, and that a tall man in the sailing ship and the personage depicted in the medallion above at the left are both Peter the Great. The ladies promenading wear fashionable costumes of the period. The palatial buildings are lavishly decorated.

59   Bed valance
Yaroslavl Province, northern Russia
Late 18th century
Whitework and drawn threadwork on linen; edging of bobbin lace with large pointed scallops
Length 178 cm (70 in), width 69 cm (27 in)
Acquired not later than 1917
Acq. No. 55215–147

The pattern is arranged with axial symmetry. The centre is occupied by a building in the arch of which a lady and gentleman are standing. The hunting scenes and plant motifs are presented heraldically.

60   Detail of panel
Late 18th century
Worked with bright coloured silks in satin stitch and long and short stitch on crimson satin
88 × 204 cm (34⅝ × 80¼ in), size of whole article
Acquired not later than 1917
Acq. No. 56770 B—94

The floral pattern with naturalistic birds is more or less regularly disposed over the whole area. The border is decorated with shellwork. The panel may be a fragment of a table covering.

233

61 Detail of a man's coat
Late 18th century
Worked with coloured silks, mainly in satin stitch and long and short stitch and with applied net on patterned velvet
Acquired in 1928
Acq. No. 62843 Б—253

Naturalistic flowers and feather-like foliage ornament the lappets, pockets and flaps of the coat. Coats were made to be left open to display the equally lavish and delicate embroidery of the waistcoat.

62 Detail of petticoat
Second half of 18th century
Worked with couched silver thread and metal strip, coloured chenille and heavy bullion on a white quilted satin ground
Acquired from the Armoury in the Moscow Kremlin in 1924
Acq. No. 55753 Р.Б.—1610

The ornamentation incorporates a chain of rich bouquets linked by a silver ribbon, made in imitation of silver lace. The robes of the 18th century had a triangular opening in the front of the skirt which allowed the petticoat to be seen. Petticoats were sometimes quilted and sometimes embroidered even more lavishly than the skirt itself.
    This petticoat was later made into a surplice.

63 Detail of a dress
Mid-18th century
Worked with coloured silks and chenille mainly in satin stitch and long and short stitch, on white satin. Decorated with applied net, silk and bird's feathers
Length 94 cm (37 in), width 44 cm (17¼ in), size of whole panel
Acquired from the P. Shchukin Collection in 1905
Acq. No. 22996 щ В—69

The fanciful pattern with its bunches of flowers, festoons and ribbons is strongly influenced by, if not directly copied from, French silks with Rococo designs.

64 Hem of ball-dress
Late 18th century
Worked with gold thread and coloured silks mainly in satin stitch on white satin. Decorated with applied net and spangles
Length 83 cm (32⅝ in), width 49 cm (19¼ in), size of whole panel
Acquired from the P. Shchukin Collection in 1905
Acq. No. 20868 щ В—73

The ornamentation of arabesques of flowers, leaves and berries is executed in pale, delicate colours. The border is patterned with interlaced foliate scrolls. Such modest and elegant embroideries on fine silks were fashionable in the late 18th and early 19th centuries.

65   Hem of ball-dress
      Last quarter of 18th century
      Worked with coloured silks in satin and stem stitch and long and short stitch and decorated with glass
      beads and with spangles
      Length 102 cm (40⅛ in), width 43 cm (16⅞ in), size of whole panel
      Acquired not later than 1917
      Acq. No. 58557 B—244

The bold repeat pattern of large-petalled flowers is separated by scrolling tendrils. The border is decorated with beadwork of geometrical character.

66   Hem of ball-dress
      Last quarter of 18th century
      Worked with coloured silks and chenille in satin stitch on white satin and decorated with spangles
      99 × 100 cm (40 × 39⅜ in), size of whole skirt
      Acquired not later than 1917
      Acq. No. 56440 B—82

The dazzling embroidery of vertical, regularly waving stems carrying ears of wheat with bows of ribbons, linked by festoons in the lower part of the hem, has an elegance characteristic of the Empire style.

67   Hem of ball-dress
      1810s
      Worked with chenille, coloured silks, wool and metal strip mainly in satin stitch on crêpe and decorated
      with spangles
      Length 80 cm (31½ in), width 50 cm (19⅝ in), size of panel
      Acquired in 1972
      Acq. No. 102568 Б—3182

The repeat pattern in reds and greens is the acanthus type of motif much in use in neoclassical ornament. The border has rosettes studded with spangles.

68   Hem of dress
      Late 18th or early 19th century
      Worked with coloured silks in satin stitch with applied net and silk
      23 × 48 cm (9 × 18⅞ in)
      Acquired in 1905
      Acq. No. 42567 B—65

Neoclassical motifs are often embroidered in colourings that are restrained, even sombre. The border pattern is of a formalized floral character, with applied woollen pompons.

69   Hem of ball-dress
      1810s
      Made by serf embroiderers

Worked with couched metal strip, chenille and beads on fine muslin
65 × 88 cm (25⅝ × 34⅝ in), size of whole panel
Acquired in 1972
Acq. No. 102568 Б—3183

The decorative motif is the European mountain ash; the background is embroidered with tiny pieces of metal strip, and the lower edge with a narrow strip of a geometrical pattern. The Empire style ball-gown typically had a high waist and narrow skirt of soft clinging muslin, with dazzling hem-embroidery that was matched on mantles and scarves. The pattern occasionally incorporated work in appliqué.

70   Detail of panel
Last quarter of 18th century
Worked with silks in satin stitch and decorated with coloured bullion, metal foil, spangles and glass beads on a satin ground
23 × 67 cm (9 × 26⅜ in), size of whole panel
Acquired not later than 1917
Acq. No. 56740 B—106

The repeat pattern is formed of spiral scrolls terminating in formalized flowers, combining reflective and matt surfaces. Such patterns were often used on the hems of dresses in the Empire style.

71   Detail of door-curtain
Late 18th or early 19th century
Worked with coloured silks and chenille in satin stitch and long and short stitch on striped satin, decorated with spangles and applied net
Length 201 cm (79 in), width 62 cm (24⅜ in), size of whole article
Acquired in 1928
Acq. No. 62791–990

Cornucopiae overflowing with flowers, baskets of flowers and exotic birds are disposed regularly over the surface. The ornamentation is strongly influenced by large-patterned French silks.

72   Handkerchief
Last quarter of 19th century
Linen decorated with whitework and drawn threadwork; edging of bobbin lace
46 × 48 cm (18 × 18⅞ in)
Acquired in 1971
Acq. No. 102207–688

The pattern is composed of shell- and scrollwork and ornamental nettings as well as naturalistic flowers. An elegant 18th-century gentleman required as accessory a hand-kerchief, sometimes called a 'neckerchief', a large square of fine linen, muslin or silk, embroidered and edged with lace.

73   Handerchief
      Late 18th century
      Lawn decorated with whitework and drawn threadwork
      37 × 38 cm (14⅝ × 15 in)
      Acquired in 1928
      Acq. No. 64357–148

The elegant, distinctly Rococo design, so popular in the second half of the 18th century, has baskets of flowers set in the corners and scrolls and floral motifs filling the border. Some thirty types of fillings are used in the small sections of the border.

74   Detail of panel
      Second half of 18th century
      Drawn threadwork and whitework applied on to a ground of red satin
      77 × 48 cm (30¼ × 18⅞ in)
      Acquired from the P. Shchukin Collection in 1905
      Acq. No. 22997 B—79

The pattern with its fanciful curving rhythms is composed of festoons worked in various types of drawn thread embroidery, a technique of needlework akin to lace-making. Since bobbin lace was extremely expensive and in short supply in the 18th century, embroidery often simulated fashionable hand-made lace.

75   Detail of quilted coverlet
      18th century
      Padded satin quilted with linen thread
      190 × 209 cm (74¾ × 82¼ in), size of whole article
      Acquired in 1965
      Acq. No. 99747 Г—838

The pattern incorporates formalized vases with floral scrolls derived from the woven patterns of the East.

76   Detail of quilted bed coverlet
      Mid-18th century
      Satin quilted with silk thread
      198 × 216 cm (77⅞ × 85 in), size of whole article
      Acquired in 1939
      Acq. No. 80256 Г—393

The ornamentation in the Rococo style, composed of various motifs, is on a ground covered all over with a swirling feather-pattern. The design is a characteristic one for Russian minor arts inspired by the Rococo.

77   Child's quilted bed coverlet
       Second half of 18th century
Satin quilted with silk thread
96 × 80 cm (37¾ × 31½ in)
Acquired in 1936
Acq. No. 78600 Г—393

The geometrical pattern of the stitching in the centrepiece is repeated on a larger scale in the outer border. The inner border is worked with curvilinear arabesques and floral designs with double palmettes.

78   Towel edge
       Late 18th century
Worked with gold thread in chain stitch on lawn cotton and decorated with spangles and moiré ribbon
Length 232 cm (91¼ in), width 39 cm (15¼ in), size of whole towel
Acquired from the P. Shchukin Collection in 1905
Acq. No. 18944 щ 124

The geometrical and foliate pattern with a large central lozenge is the Russian version of neoclassical ornament. Its modest and delicate outline-pattern is confined between moiré ribbon-borders above and below.

79   Towel edge
       Early 19th century
Worked with coloured silks in chain stitch on linen, and bordered with ribbons
Length 230 cm (90½ in), width 50 cm (19⅝ in), size of whole towel
Acquired in 1960
Acq. No. 96033 П—456

In strict axial symmetry, a vase is flanked by birds, trees and buildings. Birds in pairs hold up knotted ribbons. The inscriptions in Cyrillic letters read 'Fidelity' and 'Friendship'. The border pattern is of scrolls. Around the embroidery is a border of ribbons, and the scalloped edge is embroidered on a net ground to simulate lace. Such decorated towels were common in both towns and rural areas.

80   Towel edge
       Late 18th or early 19th century
Worked with coloured silks and metal thread in chain stitch on calico
216 × 42 cm (85 × 16½ in), size of whole towel
Acquired not later than 1890
Acq. No. 18939–23

The colour-scheme of the vase of flowers and geometrical border is modest and delicate. The ornamentation is executed entirely in chain stitch; embroidery here is being used almost as if it were drawing.

81, 82   Wedding-sheet edge
Nizhny Novgorod Province, southern Russia
Second half of 19th century
Worked with coloured linen thread in chain stitch on linen
Length 91 cm (35¾ in), width 46 cm (18⅛ in), size of whole article
Acquired not later than 1917
Acq. No. 55215

Though the sheet was in the dowry of a townswoman the motifs are those of traditional peasant embroidery, such as the Sirin-birds to bring good fortune. In accordance with the fashion of the period the women are depicted wearing long striped dresses, low-necked and decorated with floral embroidery, and large hats over centre-parted hair. Possibly the man and woman represent the betrothed pair and the two women the bridesmaids.

83   Embroidered scene
1782
Worked with coloured silk in chain and satin stitch on silk
16 × 19 cm (6¼ × 7½ in)
Acquired from the P. Shchukin Collection in 1905
Acq. No. 17499 щ Щ—47

The Chinese landscape-scene was worked by Katerina Derzhavina, wife of Gavriil Derzhavin, a Russian poet famous at the period. Chinoiserie continued to be popular until the end of the century, especially for textiles, furniture and porcelain.

84   Pocket-book cover
First quarter of 19th century
Silk embroidered with hair
10 × 15.5 cm (3⅞ × 5⅞ in)
Acquired not later than 1917
Acq. No. 58618 B—1085

The scene with sailing ships and fantastical trees is executed in fine embroidery with hair which reproduces the effect of an engraved plate. The technique was usually employed to make keepsakes.

85   Pocket-book cover
Mid-19th century
Worked with coloured silks in cross stitch on linen canvas
12.5 × 18 cm (4⅞ × 7 in)
Acquired from the P. Shchukin Collection in 1905
Acq. No. 42567 щ—144

The embroidery depicts St Basil's and the Place of Skulls on Red Square in Moscow. It is probable that the scene is based on an engraving of the 1820s. The stitching imitates the beadwork fashionable at the period.

86 Pocket-book cover
First half of 19th century
Worked with coloured silks in cross stitch on a ground of netted metal threads
10 × 14 cm (3⅞ × 5½ in)
Acquired in 1952
Acq. No. 87706 B—2374

A wreath of roses is surrounded by a wide floral border, and a narrow outer band with a formal foliate motif.

87 Rug
Late 19th century
Worked with coloured wools on canvas in cross stitch
150 × 178 cm (59 × 70 in)
Acquired in 1938
Acq. No. 79761 Г—404

Such rugs, here ornamented with naturalistically represented flowers, were commonly embroidered for sale by nuns in the convents.

88 Towel edge
Olonetsk Province, northern Russia
19th century
Counted thread work with red linen on a linen ground; edging of bobbin lace
236 × 36 cm (92⅞ × 14⅛ in)
Acquired from the I. Bilibin Collection in the 1920s
Acq. No. 54022–133

At the centre of the composition are three female figures, with double-headed eagles and small birds at either side. Above are boats and Sirin-birds. Typical of traditional Russian woodwork, this particular composition is one of the rarest in embroidery. Below are riders, and at the top is the Tree of Life motif with birds.

89 Towel edge
Nizhny Novgorod Province, northern Russia
Mid-19th century
Counted thread work with cotton and silk on a linen ground
Length 60 cm (23⅝ in), width 38 cm (15 in)
Acquired from the I. Bilibin Collection in 1922
Acq. No. 54016–1133

The stylized, symbolic motifs forming the composition include the Tree of Life and confronted panthers, their long tails terminating in flowers. The glossy pale silks used for claws, collars and the like recall Russian gold embroidery, where such details were generally worked in silver thread.

90, 92   Bed valance, and detail
Olonetsk Province, northern Russia
Mid-19th century
Counted thread work with coloured cotton and silk threads on linen.
Metal strip is used for details
Length 169 cm (66½ in), width 40 cm (15⅝ in)
Acquired in 1904
Acq. No. 42346–118

On a formalized Tree of Life perch a pair of birds with human female faces, the Alcanoste. At either side of the Tree are larger birds—the Sirin—also with female faces, and splendid plumage. Both the Sirin and the Alcanoste are birds of fable which inhabited the Russian paradise before the coming of Christianity. The small figures beside the Sirin are probably travellers lured to destruction by the birds' beautiful song. This ancient legend is not usually illustrated in the peasant embroidery of northern Russia, although the Sirin is popular as a symbol of joy and happiness, and the Alcanoste appears less frequently as a symbol of sorrow.

91   Detail of hem of skirt
Kargopol District, Olonetsk Province, northern Russia
1848
Counted thread work with linen and silk threads on linen
Length 96 cm (37⅝ in), width 40 cm (15⅝ in), size of whole panel
Acquired from the I. Bilibin Collection in the 1920s
Acq. No. 54025 B—2030

The main design is of a highly·schematicized double-headed eagle and small figures of riders, eight-petalled flowers, crosses and other geometrical motifs. The lower border is made up of a row of formalized birds.

93   Detail of bed valance
Novgorod Province, northern Russia
Mid-19th century
Worked with red linen thread in cross stitch on linen; edging of knitted lace
Length 172 cm (67⅝ in), width 23 cm (9 in), size of whole valance
Acquired in 1921
Acq. No. 52673–96

The central Tree of Life is flanked by elaborate architectural designs, each arranged with strict axial symmetry. The effect of the border, patterned with foliate and bird motifs alternating—the birds facing to the right above and to the left below—is of a clockwise motion, suggesting the succession of natural phenomena.

94   Towel edge
Vologda Province, northern Russia
Late 19th century

Worked with red cotton thread in cross stitch on linen
Length 36 cm (67⅝ in), width 23 cm (9 in)
Acquired from the I. Bilibin Collection in 1922
Acq. No. 54016–1104

Confronted peacocks, a bird motif repeated in the borders, flank a small central figure.

95   Table-cloth edging
      Bezhetsk District, Tver Province, northern Russia
      Late 19th century
      Worked with red woollen thread in cross stitch on linen; edging of machine-made lace
      Length 69 cm (27 in), width 24 cm (9⅜ in), size of whole edging
      Acquired by the Museum expedition to the Kalinin region in 1968
      Acq. No. 100823 Л–530

The repeat design is of a female figure holding solar rosettes between architectural motifs, and small birds in the interstices.

96   Wedding-sheet edge
      Novgorod Province, northern Russia
      Mid-19th century
      Worked with red linen thread in cross stitch on linen
      Length 172 cm (67⅝ in), width 45 cm (17⅝ in), size of whole edge
      Acquired in 1936
      Acq. No. 78556/96

The repeat pattern shows a *terem* (an early tent-roof house) with two seated women holding distaffs, and a Tree of Life with birds. The inspiration is undoubtedly the scenes of daily life popular in all types of peasant art. The two spinners wear horned *kichka* headdresses. The *terem* in which they sit is lavishly decorated. The frieze below the scene forms part of the architecture.

97   Towel edge
      Bezhetsk District, Tver Province, northern Russia
      1900s
      Worked with red and green woollen thread in chain stitch and counted thread work on linen
      Length 39 cm (15¼ in), width 20 cm (7⅞ in)
      Acquired by the Museum expedition to Kalinin in 1968
      Acq. No. 100823 П—529

The repeat pattern is formed of female figures holding branches (or candles?), separated by piers terminating in flowers.

98   Towel edge
      Village of Tebleshi, Tver Province, northern Russia
      Late 19th or early 20th century

Counted threadwork and drawn threadwork with linen, cotton and wool on linen
Length 37 cm (14⅝ in), width 36 cm (14⅛ in)
Acquired from the Anisimov Collection in 1931
Acq. No. 71701 B—685

The repeat pattern of male dancers is geometrical and highly stylized, yet the liveliness of the design is quite remarkable. The borders are of geometrical and plant forms.

99   Shoulder-piece of woman's blouse
     Olonetsk Province, northern Russia
     Mid-19th century
     Worked with coloured floss and twisted silks in counted thread work on linen
     14 × 26 cm (5½ × 10⅛ in)
     Acquired not later than 1917
     Acq. No. 39129–153

A central figure with arms raised has a panther at either side, the tails terminating in a flower.

100   Detail of bed valance
      Mid-19th century
      Drawn threadwork with white linen thread on linen; edging of bobbin lace
      Length 206 cm (81⅛ in), width 82 cm (32¼ in), size of whole article
      Acquired from the P. Shchukin Collection between 1905 and 1911
      Acq. No. 20923 щ—27

The ornamentation of foliage and flowers in large symmetrical scrolls resembles bobbin lace. The pattern is enclosed by bands of a simple geometrical design.

101   Towel edge
      Yaroslavl Province, southern Russia
      Early 19th century
      Drawn threadwork in linen and coloured silks; edging of bobbin lace
      Width 47 cm (18½ in)
      Acquired in 1892
      Acq. No. 26897–1029

Panthers with tails terminating in flowers and birds presented heraldically flank a Tree of Life. The narrow border is filled with geometrical motifs.

102   Towel edge
      Mid-19th century
      Worked with red cotton thread in cross stitch
      Length 230 cm (90½ in), width 38 cm (15 in), size of towel
      Acquired in 1910
      Acq. No. 46694–104

Unicorns with claw-hooves and birds flank a Tree of Life, enclosed by borders of large and small geometrical motifs.

103   End of towel
         Pskov Province, northern Russia
         Mid-19th century
Counted thread work with coloured linen and woollen threads on figured linen
Length 230 cm (90½ in), width 38 cm (15 in), size of towel
Acquired in 1895
Acq. No. 31402

The pattern of rearing horses and motifs with palmettes is reserved in plain linen and outlined in black, while the rest of the surface is worked all over in red.

104   Detail of table-cloth edging
         19th century
Satin stitch and counted thread work with coloured silks on fine linen
Length 83 cm (32⅝ in), width 16 cm (6¼ in), size of whole edging
Acquired in 1904
Acq. No. 42567

The main repeat motif is the ancient traditional one of a female figure with a horse and rider. Here, however, the representation is particularly detailed and spirited. We see the woman's apron and horned headdress, even the heels of the rider's boots. The fillings are executed in a chequered pattern.

105   Towel edge
         Vologda Province, northern Russia
         Late 19th century
Worked with red cotton thread in cross stitch and counted thread work on linen
Length 226 cm (90 in), width 36 cm (14⅛ in), size of whole towel
Acquired by the 2nd Museum expedition to northern Russia in 1929
Acq. No. 67691 Л–333

The handsome peacock is accompanied by alternating smaller birds and plant motifs. The outer border is of S-shaped scrolls, while the scalloped edging gives a very similar effect to that of bobbin lace (cf. pl. 174, top), with inverted geometricized female figures.

106   Towel ends
         Archangel Province, northern Russia
         Early 20th century
Worked with red linen thread in counted thread work on linen; edging of crochet
Length 266 cm (104⅝ in), width 35 cm (13¾ in), size of whole towel
Acquired by the Museum expedition to the Archangel region in 1972
Acq. No. 101272 Л–585

The pattern in a single colour incorporates concentric diapers and plant motifs. The bird motif in the upper part is rare in peasant embroidery and was probably derived from a printed pattern-book.

107   Fabrics for sleeves of women's shirts
      Archangel, Vologda and Olonetsk Provinces, northern Russia
      Second half of 19th century
      Worked with coloured linen, cotton and silk threads, counted thread work on linen
      Acquired from the I. Bilibin Collection in 1922
      Acq. Nos. 54018, 2033, 2035, 2040

A wide variety of decorative patterns are employed on these sleeve-pieces. Of special interest is the peacock motif incorporated into a geometricized scheme.

108   Apron
      Vologda Province, northern Russia
      Second half of 19th century
      Worked with red linen thread mainly in cross stitch on linen; edging of bobbin lace
      Length 104 cm (40 in), width 84 (33 in)
      Acquired in 1901
      Acq. No. 39306 Б—1019

border is filled with a row of panthers, birds among foliage, small human figures, swastikas and rosettes. Although the only colour used is red of a single shade, there is a great apparent variation of intensity, from the deep crimson of the lower border to the soft red-and-cream of the main part.

109   Apron
      Archangel Province, northern Russia
      Second half of 19th century
      Hem worked with woollen thread on printed calico in chain stitch
      Length 101 cm (39¾ in), width 76 cm (27⅞ in)
      Acquired by the Museum expedition to Archangel Province in 1952
      Acq. No. 83843 B—1553

The central motif is a double-headed eagle with birds and female dancers holding flowers, and the Tree of Life flanked by confronted stags. The composition is arranged in a strict axial symmetry, and bordered by narrow bands patterned with continuous scrolls.

110   Detail of bed valance
      Town of Torzhok, Tver Province, northern Russia
      Mid-19th century
      Worked with coloured linen thread in chain stitch on linen with a fringe of coarse linen threads
      Length 149 cm (59 in), width 40 cm (15⅝ in), size of whole article

Acquired not later than 1917
Acq. No. 57543–157

Peacocks flank a formalized vase with long scrolling stems carrying fruit and flowers (possibly derived from the ancient motifs of the Tree of Life and protective birds). The flowers depicted include tulips, carnations and wild roses—motifs commonly used for the gold-embroidered headdresses of the 18th century. The decoration is outstandigly attractive, especially the solid peacocks with their tails made of seven discs set on leafy stalks.

111   Towel edge
Vologda Province, northern Russia
Late 19th century
Worked with red cotton thread in chain stitch on linen
Length 34 cm (13⅜ in), width 17 cm (6⅝ in)
Acquired by the Museum expedition to northern Russia in 1929
Acq. No. 67591 B—2564

The design follows the ancient iconography of the Tree of Life motif between panthers with their tails terminating in flowers and one forepaw raised. Above and below are bird-filled bands. The scalloped edge is trimmed with a strip of red calico.

112   Towel edge
Kargopol District, Olonetsk Province, northern Russia
Late 19th or early 20th century
Worked with white cotton and coloured woollen threads in chain stitch on red calico
Length 33 cm (13 in), width 30 cm (11¾ in), size of embroidered edge
Acquired by the Museum expedition to Kargopol in 1950
Acq. No. 83206 Л–227

The motif of horse and rider with female figure is of great antiquity. In this composition the male figure on horseback is very large while the three representations of the female (once a Goddess) are very small, and to the right and left are half hidden in the ornamental scrolls. The design is outlined in white. The border is filled with simple geometrical motifs.

113   Apron hem
Kargopol District, Olonetsk Province, northern Russia
1900s
Worked with coloured linen and woollen threads mainly in chain stitch on red calico
57 × 72 cm (22⅜ × 28¼ in)
Acquired by the Museum expedition to Kargopol in 1950
Acq. No. 83206 Б—1349

An extremely formalized bird is shown in an arch of which the outline resembles a schematized double-headed eagle. The design incorporates squares, diapers, checks and zig-zags, and the border pattern is of formalized flowers.

114 Detail of bed valance
Kargopol District, Olonetsk Province, northern Russia
Early 20th century
Worked with coloured linen and woollen threads in chain and satin stitch on red calico
Length 188 cm (74 in), width 29 cm (11³⁄₈ in), size of whole valance
Acquired by the Museum expedition to Kargopol in 1950
Acq. No. 83206 B—2220

The repeat floral design is outlined in white and filled in with satin stitch of various colours.

115 Detail of hem insertion
Village of Shiryaikha, Kargopol District, Olonetsk Province, northern Russia
1900s
Worked with coloured linen, woollen and metal threads in chain and satin stitch on red calico; edging of machine-made lace
Length 78 cm (30⁵⁄₈ in), width 50 cm (19⁵⁄₈ in), size of whole article
Acquired by the Museum expedition to Kargopol in 1950
Acq. No. 83206 B—2219

The lively, naive forms and bright colours of the embroidery have something in common with Kargopol clay toy figures and whistles.

116, 117 Samplers
Voronezh and Tambov provinces, southern Russia
Second half of 19th century
Worked with coloured silks mainly in satin stitch and counted thread work
40 × 8 (15⁵⁄₈ × 3¹⁄₈); 39 × 10 (15¹⁄₄ × 3⁷⁄₈); 40 × 10 (15⁷⁄₈ × 3⁷⁄₈); 36 × 8 (14¹⁄₈ × 3¹⁄₈); 39 × 8 (15¹⁄₄ × 3¹⁄₈); 37 × 8 (14⁵⁄₈ × 3¹⁄₈)
Acquired from the I. Goriainova Collection in 1922
Acq. No. 54007

The samplers (or insertions) are all geometric patterns, worked in colourings characteristic of the Tambov and Voronezh Provinces—reds, ochres, pale blues and black. Sometimes the embroideries were in black only, the contrast being provided by the ground. The embroidered pieces might be attached to towels or be used for the backs of the *soroka* headdresses worn in southern Russia.

118 Sampler
Tambov or Voronezh Province, southern Russia
Second half of 19th century
Drawn threadwork, satin stitch and counted thread work with coloured silks on linen
12 × 12 cm (4⁵⁄₈ × 4⁵⁄₈ in)
Acquired from the I. Goriainova Collection in 1922
Acq. No. 54007–59

The interlace design is made of drawn threadwork, and the interstices are filled with geometrical motifs.

119   Detail of peasant petticoat
Orel Province, southern Russia
Early 20th century
Worked with coloured wool on woollen chequered fabric in counted thread work with spangles; edging of metal thread lace
Length 76 cm (29⅞ in), width hem 122 cm (48 in), size of whole article
Acquired by the Museum Expedition in the Orel region in 1959
Acq. No. 96

The geometric pattern is picked out with spangles, and includes saltire crosses, diamond-shapes and the like.

120   Sarafan
Kursk District, Kharkov Province, southern Russia
Second half of 19th century
Bodice embroidered with coloured wool in satin stitch and decorated with gold spangles, coloured ribbons and galloon
Length 113 cm (44½ in), width hem 228 cm (89¾ in)
Acquired not later than 1917
Acq. No. 52259 Б—471

The bodice-embroidery of this traditional Russian dress typically combines geometric and floral motifs.

121   Petticoat
Biryuchinsk District, Voronezh Province, southern Russia
Late 19th or early 20th century
Worked with coloured wool in satin stitch and a looped stitch
Length 79 cm (31⅛ in), width hem 194 cm (76⅜ in)
Acquired by the Museum expedition to the Voronezh region in 1961
Acq. No. 97480

A peasant woman's petticoat has satin stitch and looped stitches outlining the chequered pattern of the fabric.

122   Back of woman's shirt
Ostrogozhsk District, Voronezh Province, southern Russia
Early 20th century
Worked with black linen thread in counted thread work on linen
Length 64 cm (25⅛ in), width 154 cm (60⅝ in)
Acquired by the Museum expedition to the Voronezh region in 1956
Acq. No. 92003 Б—1868

Geometric motifs border the shoulder-pieces and the cuffs of red calico. Black embroidery was popular for the decoration of women's festive shirts in two areas only—the Tambov and Voronezh Provinces of Russia.

THE LACE

123   Detail of chalice-cover edge
17th century
Bobbin lace of gold and silver thread
Width 5 cm (2 in), edging only
Acquired from the Church of the Intercession of the Virgin at Fili, Moscow, in 1941
Acq. No. Р.Б.—4311/80965

The repeat design is a stylized carnation on an irregular diamond-shaped mesh ground.
The broad scallops are outlined with a zig-zag line. The fact that the edging is sewn to
the chalice-cover with the scalloped edge outwards is unusual in a 17th-century textile.

124   Braid on ecclesiastical vestment
17th century
Bobbin lace of gold thread
Width 5 cm (2 in)
Acquired from the Kostroma Museum in 1933
Acq. No. Р.Б.—2591/75323

The pattern is a regular lattice, decorated throughout with picots. Similar lace edgings
were occasionally decorated with pearls. (Cf. pl. 162 for a similarly made linen lace.)

125   Edging of phelonion
17th century
Bobbin lace of silver thread
Width 11 cm (4¼ in)
Acquired from the Museum in Alexandrova Sloboda in 1930
Acq. No. Р.Б.—2296/68988

The repeat floral motif has a large-scale mesh ground. Different thicknesses of thread are
used to introduce relief. The large scallops are delineated by a double row of 'wheat-
grains' or 'leaves', a feature characteristic of 17th-century Russian lace.

126   Chalice-cover edge
17th century
Bobbin lace of gold and silver thread
Width of edging 8 cm (3⅛ in)
Acquired from the Alexandrova Sloboda Museum in 1930
Acq. No. Р.Б.—2142/6905

The highly formalized floral pattern is mainly in tape lace with joining bars and some mesh ground. The scalloped edge is outlined with a separate wavy trail. In the 17th-century edgings, as here, were usually sewn on to fabric with their scalloped edge turned inward. The rich texture of the edgings was accentuated with linings of contrasting colours.

127, 128   Shroud edge
First half (pl. 127) and middle (pl. 128) of 18th century
Gimp lace of gold and silver thread, gold gimp and metal strip
Width 8 cm (3¹⁄₈ in), each
Acquired from the Vysoko-Petrovsky Monastery in 1924
Acq. Nos. Г-106/55695, Г-105/55695

The designs are based on intricate tracery of rich scrolls, with picots, net fillings and a bold, firm gimp emphasizing the pattern. Similar lace continued in popularity until the 19th century.

129   Chalice-cover edge
Mid-18th century
Tape lace of silver and gold thread, with addition of silver gimp
Width 8 cm (3¹⁄₈ in)
Acquired from the Alexandrova Sloboda Museum in 1930
Acq. No. Р.Б.—5011/68981

The repeat-motif of a floral character has a rosette in the centre, composed of small compact ovals called 'wheat-grains' or 'leaves'. In the later 18th and 19th centuries the rosette was superseded by a five- or seven-petalled flower, which became conventional in Russian folk art generally. The straight edge is defined by a line of narrow interlacing bands.

130   Insertion
18th century
Bobbin lace of silver thread
Width 3 cm (1¹⁄₈ in)
Acquired from the P. Schukin Collection between 1905 and 1911
Acq. No. 3–472/20854 щ

The design incorporates rosettes made of 'wheat-grains' and plain ovals and roundels, arranged regularly on a loose mesh ground. As the outer edges have only tiny scallops, the lace could serve either as an insertion or as an edging.

131   Top: Galloon
18th century
Bobbin lace of gold thread, with addition of gold strip
Width 10 cm (3⁷⁄₈ in)
Acquired from Moscow University in 1936
Acq. No. 3–643/78014

The continuous waving trail is outlined with parallel 'strings of pearls'. The curves on each side are filled with fan motifs in gold strip. The lace could serve as an insertion or as an edging.

Centre and bottom: Galloons
18th century
Bobbin lace of silver thread, with addition of silver strip
Width 5 cm (2 in), 7 cm (2⅝ in)
Acquired from the Stroganov Art College, Moscow, and the State Museum Reserve in 1939
Acq. Nos. 3–373/531142, 3–860/80076

Both designs include fan motifs and 'wheat-grains'. Such patterns were widely popular in the 18th century.

132   Edging
Second half of 18th century
Bobbin lace of gold, silver and coloured metal strip
Width 7 cm (2⅝ in)
Acquired from the Moscow Region Museum Reserve in 1938
Acq. No. 3–901/79836

The repeat pattern is a broad waving band with fan motifs below, and rosettes of 'wheat-grains'. Each meander of the central trail is connected to the straight edge, or footside.
    Such rich laces were employed for both peasant festive garments and ecclesiastical vestments, but rarely for the costumes of the nobility.

133   Bed valance insertion
Late 18th century
Bobbin lace of silver thread and silver strip
Width 21 cm (8¼ in)
Acquired from the P. Shchukin Collection between 1905 and 1911
Acq. No. 3–723/20577 щ

The repeat design is of plain and stepped lozenges with fillings and rosettes of 'wheat-grains' alternating on a regular square mesh ground. The motifs are outlined with a heavier silver thread. The borders are decorated with series of small scallops. Bed linen in the 19th century was usually decorated with such geometrical patterns.

134   Detail of scarf
Mid-18th century
Bobbin lace of silver thread with addition of silver strip
Width 36 cm (14⅛ in)
Acquired in 1937
Acq. No. 3–888/78959

Large foliate motifs alternate with smaller diamond-shaped medallions with dense fillings of 'wheat-grains', on a fine mesh ground. The pattern is outlined with a silver strip, and small rosettes of silver strip add further ornament. The straight edge is bordered with tiny fans, the fancy edge with large oval scallops.

135   Towel end with co-ordinated insertion and edging
Second half of 18th century
Tape lace of coloured silks, white linen and gold thread
Width 38.5 cm (15⅛ in)
Acquired as a gift in 1890
Acq. No. Kp. 6.—122/19884

Both ends of the towel have a lace insertion and edging separated by a silk ribbon. On the insertion a formalized double-headed eagle is flanked by peacocks and flowers. The edging is filled with formalized leaf motifs. The continuous pattern of tape lace is highlighted with fine gold thread. The mesh fillings are worked in coloured silks, their browns and pinks harmonizing with the coarse white linen and fine gold thread. This combination of different materials in a single piece is characteristic of 18th-century lace. The towel on to which the lace is sewn is of green silk taffeta. Such towels, popular in merchants' households, were purely ornamental.

136   Detail of insertion
Late 18th or early 19th century
Bobbin lace of gold thread
Width 12 cm (4⅝ in)
Acquired from the Department of Museum Affairs in 1925
Acq. No. 3–274/56738

The repeat design is of diamonds with a variety of fillings based on *brides picotées*. The loose diamond-shaped ground mesh is typical of 18th-century lace. The composition and use of picots were inspired by lace of linen and cotton thread.

137   Towel edging
Late 18th century
Tape lace of black silk, gold and silver thread
Length 43 cm (16⅞ in), width 7 cm (2⅝ in)
Acquired through the State Purchasing Commission in 1944
Acq. No. 3–997/81403

Formalized peacocks and double-headed eagles alternate, their gold thread fillings decorated with picots, and their outlines worked in a heavier gold thread for emphasis against the regular mesh ground of silver thread. The exquisite interplay of gold, silver and black silk threads creates an effect of jewel-like richness.

138   Detail of insertion
18th century
Tape lace of coloured silks and gold thread
Width 8 cm (3⅛ in)
Acquired from the P. Shchukin Collection between 1905 and 1911
Acq. No. 3–240/20595 щ

A formalized leaf pattern is bordered with bands of tape lace. The leaves of pink and green silk alternate with leaves of gold thread. Each motif joins directly to the next, without any ground at all. With the addition of coloured silks, lace which had formerly been heavy and elaborate in design gradually became lighter and more elegant.

139   Detail of bed valance
Galich, Kostroma Province
Late 18th century
Bobbin lace of coloured silks and white linen thread
Width 24.5 cm (9⅝ in)
Acquired in 1922
Acq. No. 3–736/53138

The insertion consists of scrolls containing formal leaf motifs in a typical Rococo design —light, graceful and asymmetrical. The edging repeats the leaf motifs. The scalloped edge is emphasized with a band of cloth stitch. The unbleached linen thread of the regular mesh ground tones with the pale silks of the ornamentation. The pattern of the insertion is emphasized by heavier grey-blue and pink threads. The main design of the insertion, winding scrolls, is outlined with gold thread. A rhythmical effect is created by the grey-blues, golden yellows and pinks of the edging.

140   Detail of bed valance
Galich, Kostroma Province
Late 18th century
Bobbin lace of coloured silks, white linen and gold threads
Width 15 cm (5⅞ in)
Acquired in 1922
Acq. No. 3–714/53138

The repeat pattern of the insertion is based on a winding chain of ovals, inset with little leaves, with floral springs filling the spaces above and below. The edging has a smaller meander and slightly different springs bordered with small roundels and shallow chevrons. The ground is a large-scale hexagonal mesh.

141   Detail of bed valance, co-ordinated insertion and edging
Galich, Kostroma Province
Late 18th or early 19th century
Bobbin lace of coloured silks, white linen thread and gold thread
Width 28 cm (11 in)
Acquired from the P. Shchukin Collection between 1905 and 1911
Acq. No. 3–713/20596 щ

The insertion ornament consists of figured medallions with various fillings, alternating with formalized floral sprigs; the edging is a continuous line of festoons with ornamental grounds below and floral motifs above, while the edge itself is of roundels and shallow chevrons. Outlining the patterns is a heavier coloured silk or gold thread. The effect of the solid areas of coloured silks is enhanced by the contrast they form with the regularity of the net ground of fine linen thread.

142   Towel edge
Galich, Kostroma Province
Late 18th or early 19th century
Bobbin lace of white linen thread and gold thread
39 × 51 cm (15¼ × 20 in)
Acquired as a gift in 1887
Acq. No. Кр. 6.—64/15894

The motif of the insertion is a stylized Tree of Life with protective birds represented in heraldic style, carried out in a heavier linen thread on a fine diagonal mesh ground. The birds occur again in the edging pattern outlined with gold thread. The shaped edge is finished with a narrow band of cloth stitch.

143   Detail of towel edge
Galich, Kostroma Province
Late 18th or early 19th century
Bobbin lace of coloured silks, white linen thread and gold thread
Length 98.5 cm (38¾ in), width 32 cm (12⅝ in), size of whole towel
Acquired from the P. Shchukin Collection between 1905 and 1911
Acq. No. Кр. 6.—6/20283 щ

The insertion pattern is of stylized bird and foliate motifs; the edging is of similar motifs with pairs of flying birds. The border is finished with a narrow band of cloth stitch. The silk ornamental motifs vary in tone from a greenish shade to pink to yellow, and are outlined with gold thread. The fine diagonal mesh ground is of linen thread.

144   Detail of bed valance
Galich, Kostroma Province
Early 19th century
Bobbin lace of coloured silks and white linen thread
Width 37.5 cm (14¾ in)
Acquired in 1922
Acq. No. 3–737/53138

The insertion repeat design is of highly formalized leaf motifs. In the edging a similar motif alternates with stylized birds. The scalloped edge has a band of tape lace. The fine diagonal mesh ground of semi-bleached linen thread is in contrast with the green and yellow silks.

145   Detail of bed valance
       Galich, Kostroma Province
       Early 19th century
       Bobbin lace of coloured silks and white linen thread
       Width 25 cm (9¾ in)
       Acquired from the P. Shchukin Collection between 1905 and 1911
       Acq. No. Кр. б.—858/20619 щ

The ornamentation of the insertion, typical of peasant embroidery, is the one of the traditional Tree of Life motif flanked by confronted horses. In the edging, confronted birds are separated by diamonds with different fillings; the shaped edge is emphasized by cloth stitch in zig-zags. The motifs are executed in white linen thread and outlined with beige and green silks on a diagonal mesh ground.

146   Detail of bed valance
       Galich, Kostroma Province
       Early 19th century
       Bobbin lace of coloured silks and white linen thread
       Width 30 cm (11¾ in)
       Acquired in 1922
       Acq. No. 3–719/53138

The conventional composition of the insertion is of a Tree of Life with peacocks and smaller birds. The edging pattern has formalized human and animal motifs. The fancy border is edged with a zig-zag band of cloth stitch. The mesh ground is of fine white linen thread, and is basically a diamond mesh, with areas of hexagonal mesh and larger holes. The ornamentation of the insertion is of palest blue-green and yellow silk thread, and the edging pattern is predominantly of pale blues, greens and yellows. Some elements are made of twisted silk two-colour thread, a feature peculiar to Galich lace.

147   Detail of bed valance
       Galich, Kostroma Province
       Early 19th century
       Bobbin lace of coloured silks, white linen thread and gold thread
       Width 35 cm (13¾ in)
       Acquired from the P. Shchukin Collection between 1905 and 1911
       Acq. No. 3–725/2099

The insertion shows a delicate waving line carrying leaves and flowers; the edging pattern incorporates a row of stags, widely separated and alternating with vases of flowers. Cartouches with open-work fillings decorate the fancy border. The mesh ground is of fine white linen thread. The pattern, in blue-green, yellow and pink silks, is outlined with a gold thread. The use of a thick gold outline-thread rather than a heavy linen or silk thread is characteristic of Galich lace.

148   Detail of insertion
       Galich, Kostroma Province
       19th century
       Bobbin lace of white linen thread
       Width 21 cm (8¼ in)
       Acquired through the State Purchasing Commission in 1928
       Acq. No. Kp. 6.—169/64704

The peacock motif is outlined in a heavier linen thread for clearer definition against the coarse net ground. This ornamental motif was very popular in the Russian decorative arts generally, and particularly so in peasant embroidery.

149   Detail of insertion
       19th century
       Bobbin lace of white linen thread
       Width 13 cm (5⅛ in)
       Acquired in 1922
       Acq. No. 397/53138

The evenly worked mesh ground provides a contrast with the scattered bird motifs, carried out in cloth stitch, all in fine linen thread.

150   Towel edging
       Vologda Province
       First half of 19th century
       Tape lace of linen and silver thread
       Width 31 cm (12⅛ in)
       Acquired in 1922
       Acq. No. 3–33/53138

A silver gimp thread runs through the curves of the vermiculated design. The tape lace is joined by the brides without any ground. Ornamentation is added by a large-scale mesh filling of silver thread and rosettes of 'wheat-grains'. The scalloped edge has an openwork, toothed border of linen. The silvery colouring combined with the gradation of tone of the linen thread, bleached less strongly to give a darker shade, creates an unusual and elegant effect.

151   Detail of wedding-sheet valance
       Vologda Province
       Late 18th century
       Tape lace of white linen, coloured silk, gold and metal threads
       Width 63.5 cm (25 in)
       Acquired through the State Purchasing Board in 1909
       Acq. No. Kp. 6.—2/45799

The valance is composed of a lace insertion and edging separated by a band, also of lace, in gold thread. The large conventionalized floral motifs of the insertion are repeated in the edging. The outlines of the motifs are emphasized with a heavier linen thread, and they are joined by a variety of net grounds, worked in silks of pale blue, pink, yellow and green. The flowers' centres are worked in the same colours or with metal thread. The variety of colours of the fillings creates a pleasing rhythmical effect. The use of colour is not, however, generally characteristic of Vologda lace. The border is outlined with a separate, wavy, tape lace strip. The gold thread insertion is composed of two waving bands, the spaces filled alternately with rosettes of 'wheat-grains' and cloth stitch.

152   Detail of wedding-sheet valance
Vologda Province
Late 18th or early 19th century
Tape lace of white linen thread
Width 42.5 cm (16⅝ in)
Acquired through the Museum Purchasing Commission in 1929
Acq. No. Kp. 6.—162/58602

The convoluted floral repeat pattern of tape lace almost completely fills the area of both insertion and edging. The centres of the stylized flowers contain a ground of 'wheat-grains', and rosettes are dotted in the smaller spaces. The narrow borders have a geometrical pattern, its motif repeated in the footside of the edging.

153   Detail of insertion
Vologda Province, northern Russia
First half of 19th century
Tape lace of white linen thread
Width 11 cm (4⅓ in)
Acquired from the P. Shchukin Collection between 1905 and 1911
Acq. No. 3–926/18935 щ

Each section of the stylized design shows a formalized Tree of Life flanked by confronted peacocks presented in the heraldic manner. There is some irregular mesh ground. The linear and curving pattern is typical of Vologda lace.

154   Detail of sheet valance
Yaroslavl Province
Second half of 18th century
Tape lace of white linen thread
Width 40 cm (15⅝ in)
Acquired from the P. Shchukin Collection between 1905 and 1911
Acq. No. C—50/20616 щ

The floral forms in the insertion design are joined by irregular *brides picotées*. The tape laces widen to accommodate various fillings in the Rococo style, of asymmetrical and freely shaped scrolls. The edging pattern contains somewhat more formal foliate motifs.

155   Insertion
Vologda Province
First half of 19th century
Tape lace of white linen thread
Length 31 cm (12⅛ in), width 18 cm (7 in)
Acquired in 1924
Acq. No. 3–935/54776

A pair of confronting panthers, each with a forepaw raised, is defined by the tape lace against the coarse mesh ground. The design is outlined with thick linen thread running through a tape lace band.

    The conventionalized animal motif was widely used in the ornamentation of Vologda lace.

156   Detail of towel edging
Rostov the Great, Yaroslav
First half of 19th century
Tape lace of white linen thread
Width 25 cm (9¾ in)
Acquired from the P. Shchukin Collection between 1905 and 1911
Acq. No. 3–126/20594 щ

The insertion has a schematized eagle flanked by confronted peacocks; the edging design incorporates a many-petalled flower. The portions of the pattern are joined by brides decorated with picots forming a squared ground. A heavy thread is used in the centre of the tape for a raised effect.

157   Detail of sheet valance
Vologda Province
First half of 19th century
Tape lace of white linen thread
Width 38 cm (15 in)
Acquired from the P. Shchukin Collection between 1905 and 1911
Acq. No. C—45/20572

The wide band of geometrical-pattern drawn threadwork is edged with lace of conventionalized foliate motifs. The vermiculated pattern of tape lace is punctuated by rosettes and areas filled entirely with 'wheat-grains'. The scallops are outlined with a narrow band of loosely worked cloth stitch.

158   Detail of sheet valance (cf. detail of lace, p. 149)
Nizhny Novgorod Province
First half of 19th century
Tape lace of white linen thread
Width 56 cm (22 in)
Acquired from the P. Shchukin Collection between 1905 and 1911
Acq. No. C—45/20604 щ

The insertion is decorated with the traditional motifs of the Tree of Life flanked by confronted peacocks and double-headed eagles. The scallops of the border are filled with a vermiculated design of formalized floral and foliate forms. The tape lace incorporates a thicker thread, and the ground is a diagonal mesh. The bold, elaborate design, the use of relief, the large rosettes of 'wheat-grains' and the fancy fillings are all characteristic features of Nizhny Novgorod lace-making.

159   Detail of sheet valance
Nizhny Novgorod Province
First half of 19th century
Tape lace of white linen thread
Width 56 cm (22 in.)
Acquired from the P. Shchukin Collection between 1905 and 1911
Acq. No. Кр. б.—145/20604 щ

Formalized vases with plants rising from them symmetrically are alternated with foliate motifs for the insertion. Similar foliate motifs make up the scalloped edge. The tape lace sections of the design are joined by a fancy mesh ground. The thick outlining thread, raised rosettes of 'wheat-grains' and varied grounds all contribute to the creation of a highly decorative effect.

160   Detail of edging
Yelets, Orel Province
19th century
Bobbin lace of white cotton thread
Width 12 cm (4⅝ in)
Acquired from the P. Shchukin Collection between 1905 and 1911
Acq. No. 3—91/20591 щ

The arches of formalized leaves are closed below by a chain of open rings, and are filled with floral sprigs. Two sizes of hexagonal mesh are used, the smaller in the motif and the larger for the main ground area. Both ground and motifs, outlined with a thick glossy thread, are extremely precisely worked.

161   Detail of edging
Yelets, Orel Province
Second half of 19th century
Bobbin lace of white cotton thread
Width 19 cm (7½ in)
Acquired through the Museum Purchasing Commission in 1964
Acq. No. 3–1319/98884

The repeat design, rather similar in character to that of the preceding plate (pl. 160), is of floral wreaths filled with an openwork net ground on a thin, fine mesh ground. The pattern is outlined with a shiny, heavy thread, and stands out boldly against a fine hexagonal net ground. Tiny open rings and filled circles border the scalloped edge.

162 Detail of insertion
Yelets, Orel Province
19th century
Bobbin lace of white cotton thread
Width 7.5 cm (2⅞ in)
Acquired as a gift in 1956
Acq. No. 3–1326/100098

The pattern consists of a regular, diamond-shaped mesh known in Russia as 'pearl netting'. Little roundels of cloth stitch are linked by a trellis pattern, a design which could be interpreted as representing the effect of pearls or beads sewn on to a net ground. Each of the four sides of the lozenge is decorated with a solid roundel of tape lace.

163 Detail of edging
Yelets, Orel Province
Mid-19th century
Bobbin lace of white linen thread
Width 12.5 cm (4⅞ in)
Acquired through the State Purchasing Board in 1899
Acq. No. 3–991/36454

The design of foliate and geometrical motifs in cloth stitch, outlined with a thick, glossy thread, shows an imaginative variety of openwork grounds. The lace is edged with a row of small diamond-shapes and a band of solid cloth stitch.

164 Detail of edging
Yelets, Orel Province
19th century
Bobbin lace of white linen thread
Width 6 cm (2⅜ in)
Acquired as a gift in 1923
Acq. No. 3–76/54657

The design is formed of series of roundels and simple trefoil motifs arranged in three staggered rows on a fine net ground. The lace is of Valenciennes type, characterized by a regular, diamond-shaped mesh ground and a floral pattern without an outlining thread. The absence of a heavy outlining thread meant that it was easy to launder, and hence it was generally preferred for trimming personal linen.

165 Detail of insertion
Yelets, Orel Province
Early 20th century
Bobbin lace of black cotton thread
Width 7 cm (2⅝ in)
Acquired through the State Purchasing Commission in 1966
Acq. No. 3–1332/99881

The pattern is of rosettes of elongated 'wheat-grains', connected by brides decorated with picots, without any ground at all.

166 Handkerchief border
Yelets, Orel Province
Late 19th or early 20th century
Bobbin lace of white cotton thread
34 × 34 cm (13³⁄₈ × 13³⁄₈ in), size of trimmed handkerchief
Acquired from the Stroganov Art College in 1928
Acq. No. 3–814/64353

The clear, elegant design is composed of ornamental scrolls, foliate motifs, chains and honeycomb fillings, outlined by a thick glossy thread on a fine mesh ground. This Russian lace is similar in style to English Buckinghamshire lace.

167 Mat border
Yelets, Orel Province
Late 19th or early 20th century
Bobbin lace; white cotton thread
Diam. 24.5 cm (9⁵⁄₈ in), whole mat
Acquired through the Purchasing Board in 1964
Acq. No. 3–1315/98884

The elements of the pattern are linked by large areas of brides decorated with picots. The thick thread and areas of 'half stitch', which is less dense than cloth stitch, are characteristic of Russian lace-making in the late 19th and early 20th centuries. The large number of raised leaves on the half stitch areas, and the rosettes and *brides picotées*, are also typical of English Bedfordshire lace.

168, 169 Coverlet corner and detail of centrepiece
Yelets, Orel Province
Late 19th century
Bobbin lace, worked in strips and then joined; cream-coloured linen thread
255 × 258 cm (100³⁄₈ × 101⁵⁄₈ in), size of whole item
Acquired from the State Purchasing Commission in 1950
Acq. No. 3–1032/82743

Floral rosettes and plant motifs appear as outlines in heavier linen thread on a fine mesh ground with contrasted fillings. The scallops are bordered with openwork roundels. The design is outlined with a heavier linen thread. The *boteh* (vase and flowers) motif of Eastern derivation was popular in the second half of the 19th century, and was used for the ornamentation of woven textiles and for embroidery as well as for lace.

170 Detail of insertion
Mtsensk, Orel Province
Late 19th or early 20th century
Width 9 cm (3½ in)
Acquired from the Lace Collection of the Mtsensk District, Orel Province, in 1924
Acq. No. 3–971/55628

The row of open hexagons with fancy fillings is punctuated by floral motifs arranged vertically, on a closely worked mesh ground. The pattern is outlined with a heavier thread.

171 Detail of edging
Mtsensk, Orel Province
Second half of 19th century
Bobbin lace of white linen and cotton threads
Width 14.5 cm (5⅝ in)
Acquired through the State Purchasing Board in 1963
Acq. No. 3–1310/96130

The geometrical pattern is displayed on an unusual mesh ground. A heavier cotton thread delineates the motifs, creating a secondary design which harmonizes with the main pattern. The footside is decorated with wavy openwork and a zig-zag band of cloth stitch.

172 Detail of edging
Vyatka Province
Late 19th century
Straight lace of unbleached linen and white cotton thread
Width 20 cm (7⅞ in)
Acquired through the State Purchasing Board in 1962
Acq. No. 3–1280/96238

Geometricized plant motifs on a large hexagonal mesh are set in each diamond, and are repeated in the spaces between the diamonds on the straight edge. The pattern is outlined with a coarse, twisted white thread. The scallops are bordered with a band of cloth stitch and a looped edging.

173 Fragment of edging
Town of Kalyazin, Tver Province
Second half of 19th century
Tape lace of white linen thread
Width 12 cm (4⅝ in)
Acquired in 1925
Acq. No. 3–914/56509

The bobbin tape lace forming a foliate pattern is joined to itself by bars, leaving areas of fancy mesh ground. Tape lace of close texture and a limited use of mesh give this edging a heavy, bold appearance.

174 Details of edgings
Mikhailov District, Ryazan Province
19th century
Lace of white linen and coloured cotton threads
Width 4 cm (1⅝ in), 6.5 cm (2½ in), 7 cm (2⅝ in)
Acquired from the State Museum Reserve in 1924
Acq. Nos. 3–932/54776, 3–1056/55629, 3–496/69722

These edgings with pronounced semi-circular scallops are decorated with geometrical patterns of red and white threads, traditional for peasant lace. They are made without a pricked pattern.

175 Details of edgings
Mikhailov District, Ryazan Province
19th century
Lace of white linen and coloured cotton threads
Width 1.5 cm (⅝ in), 5 cm (2 in), 6.5 cm (2½ in)
Acquired from the State Museum Reserve in 1924
Acq. Nos. 3–938/54776, 3–922/56509, 3–934/54776

These geometrical patterns of bands, triangles and zig-zags are characteristic of peasant lace made without a pricked pattern.

176 Detail of insertion
Kherson Province
First quarter of 19th century
Made by serf lace-makers
Straight lace of white linen thread
Width 11 cm (4¼ in)
Acquired through the Museum Purchasing Commission in 1972
Acq. No. 3–1440/102569

The pattern shows a series of geometrical rosettes with ornamental fillings on a fine net ground. Is is a Mechlin type of lace, readily distinguished by the presence of a thick glossy thread outlining the motifs. Light in appearance and gossamer-fine, it was commonly used as an edging for muslin gowns, and for frills.

177 Detail of edging
Kherson Province
First half of 19th century
Made by serf lace-makers
Bobbin lace of white linen thread
Width 14 cm (5½ in)
Acquired through the State Purchasing Board in 1972
Acq. No. 3–1141/102569

This lace of the Mechlin type has a graceful design similar to whitework embroidery.

Sprays of flowers and leaves in each scallop are outlined with a shiny thread, and displayed on a fine mesh ground of round holes, with small dots on the field.

178 Detail of scarf
First half of 19th century
Bobbin lace of cream-coloured silk thread
Length 160 cm (63 in), width 61 cm (24 in)
Acquired through the Museum Purchasing Commission in 1962
Acq. No. 3–1281/98054

The design is of large bouquets of flowers in the border and small sprig-motifs dispersed in the field on a very fine net ground. The lace is made from filmy, natural-coloured Chinese floss silk, with the motifs outlined by a narrow strip of tape lace and glossy raised thread. The dense areas of the pattern form a strong contrast with the almost transparent mesh ground.

179 Shawl of blonde lace
1820s
Bobbin lace of cream-coloured silk thread
Length 250 cm (98¾ in), width 20 cm (7⅞ in)
Acquired as a gift in 1905
Acq. No. Б–153/42798

The piece is bordered with large floral and foliate motifs and a line of small flowers. The solid elements of the pattern are worked in and also outlined by a thicker shiny thread against an almost transparent net ground.

180 Detail of collar of blonde lace
Mid-19th century
Bobbin lace of white silk and gold thread
Width 17.5 cm (6⅞ in)
Acquired from the Brocard Collection in 1924
Acq. No. 3–708/55142

Floral scrolls in cloth stitch with fancy fillings are set against a fine hexagonal ground. The main elements of the pattern are outlined with a gold thread. This type of lace was sometimes made of black, gold or silver thread.

181 Trimming for neck of dress
Second half of 19th century
Bobbin lace of black silk thread
Length 302 cm (118⅞ in), width 38 cm (15 in)
Acquired in 1928
Acq. No. 3–785/62764

The main portion of the collar, which is divided into four compartments, and the tear-drop shaped areas in the ties, have a filling of *brides picotées* and cameo-like medallions containing vine-leaves. Bands of pattern define the compartments and border. The outer edge and the tie ends of the collar are finished with small scallops, each one containing a rosette.

Glossary

Embroidery

APPLIED WORK, APPLIQUÉ

A form of embroidery in which designs are created by stitching a fabric or embroidered motif on to a contrasting ground.

BASKET STITCH

A couched thread technique by which the effect produced is of basket-weave.

BULLION

Tightly coiled metal thread.

CHAIN STITCH

Stitch worked with a needle or hook (when it is also called tambour stitch). It is used as an outline stitch, or to cover large areas rapidly.

CHENILLE

A tufted velvety thread used for trimming and embroidery.

CROSS STITCH

A counted thread stitch (q.v.), normally worked in blocks.

COUCHED WORK

A technique in which thread is laid on the ground material and stitched to it with a fine thread, usually of another type. It is used where the main thread is thick and would damage the ground if pulled through, and/or where a thread is too precious to waste by being carried underneath the fabric.

COUNTED THREAD WORK

Embroidery worked on an even-weave fabric, counting the number of threads over which a stitch is made. This method produces a regular, geometric pattern, which is often reversible.

DRAWN THREADWORK

Embroidery in which threads are pulled out of the fabric and the pattern is darned on to the remaining threads, usually with thread of type similar to that of the ground fabric.

FIGURED

A term used to describe a textile decorated with figures, flowers, fruit etc.

FLOSS SILK

A soft, untwisted silk thread.

FOIL	A thin sheet of metal, used in embroidery to create the effect of precious stones.
GIMP	A thread which is very highly twisted, so as to be very firm and round.
HAIR EMBROIDERY	Fine embroidery with black silk or hair, imitating the effect of engraved prints.
KOKOSHNIK	One of the many types of elaborate headdresses of Russia. It was considered immodest for a married lady to show her hair.
LONG AND SHORT STITCH	Stitches used to obtain a smooth, densely covered surface in which many shades may be introduced, producing a gradual change of colour.
METAL STRIP	A thin and narrow strip of metal used in embroidery.
METAL THREAD	A narrow and very thin strip of metal wound around a silk core. The pliable thread which results is easier to work than metal strip.
MOIRÉ	A weave which produces a watery appearance on the surface of a fabric.
PHELONION	A liturgical vestment worn by all officiating Orthodox priests—the equivalent of a chasuble in the Catholic Church.
QUILTING	The decorative stitching together of several thicknesses of material.
RAISED WORK	Relief, or three-dimensional embroidery created by working over small wooden or cardboard shapes, or over pads of cotton or wool.
SATIN STITCH	A double-sided stitch giving a dense, smooth, satin-like appearance.
SHIRINKA TOWEL	A large ceremonial towel or kerchief carried in the hand, an indispensable accessory for occasions such as a wedding.
SPANGLE	A small disc of shiny metal or similar reflective material.

SPLIT-STITCH	Stitch used to obtain a fine, controlled line. It was used frequently in ecclesiastical embroidery to model the face, hands and limbs of figures.
STEM STITCH	A line stitch used in many kinds of floral embroidery.
VALANCE	Hanging drapery, usually the edge of bed-hangings, curtains or tablecloths.
WHITEWORK	Embroidery using white thread on a white ground.

Lace

BLONDE LACE	A fine silk bobbin lace with a hexagonal mesh ground, and with the design carried out in thicker, floss silk. Originally it was cream-coloured, but later black silk was used as well. (cf. pl. 36)
BRIDE	A bar of thread worked to join the elements of the pattern together, especially where there is no mesh ground. Sometimes the brides are decorated with picots, when they are called *brides picotées*.
CHANTILLY LACE	A very fine black or white silk lace with hexagonal mesh ground. Each element of the pattern is outlined with a thicker strand of flat untwisted silk, instead of with more usual twisted outline thread.
CLOTH STITCH	A structure identical to plain weave made in bobbin lace.
CLUNY LACE	A rather coarse type of lace made in the late 19th century in France (at Mirecourt in Lorrain, and Le Puy).
EDGING	Lace with one straight edge and one fancy or scalloped border.
FILET EMBROIDERY or *LACIS*	Embroidery on a foundation of square meshes, either made as a net or formed by drawn threads, in which some squares are filled in with stitches to form the design.

267

FLOSS SILK	A soft, untwisted silk thread, used especially in blonde lace.
FOOTSIDE	The straight edge of a piece of lace; the side which will be sewn to the material it is to decorate.
GALLOON	A braid or lace with identical scalloping along both borders, symmetrical about the centre line.
GIMP	A thread which is very highly twisted, so as to be very firm and round. It is used to outline and emphasize parts of the design.
GUIPURE LACE	In general, lace in which the elements of the pattern are joined by brides (q.v.), without any mesh ground at all.
INSERTION	A band of lace with two straight edges or footsides, made for the purpose of sewing between two pieces of material.
LACIS	*See* Filet embroidery.
MECHLIN LACE	A straight lace with a hexagonal mesh ground, and the design motifs outlined with a gimp thread (q.v.).
PICOT	A loop of thread formed during the working of the lace, often on the sides of brides (q.v.).
STRAIGHT LACE	Lace in which the motifs and the mesh ground are worked at the same time, with the same threads taking part in both motif and ground.
TAPE LACE	A narrow band of cloth stitch made as the lace progresses, which often forms a linear design that doubles back on itself, and is joined to itself either directly or with brides (q.v.). A mesh ground may be added later, or worked at the same time.
VALENCIENNES LACE	A straight lace (q.v.), usually with a pronounced diamond-shaped mesh ground, characterized by the absence of an outlining thread around the pattern motifs, which are usually small flowers or sprigs.
'WHEAT-GRAINS' or LEAVES	Small compact ovals worked at regular intervals in the ground, or grouped together in a rosette- or flower-shape.

Index Numbers in italic refer to the plates

THE EMBROIDERY